Family Literacy Works

The NFER evaluation of the Basic Skills Agency's Demonstration Programmes

———

GREG BROOKS • TOM GORMAN
JOHN HARMAN • DOUGAL HUTCHISON • ANNE WILKIN

© The Basic Skills Agency
7th Floor, Commonwealth House, 1-19 New Oxford Street, London WC1A 1NU.
Published March 1996
ISBN 1 85990 047 X
Design: Studio 21

Contents

———

Chapter

List of Tables

List of Figures

Abbreviations

LEA   Local Education Authority

N   sample size

NCDS   National Child Development Study; in this report, this almost always means specifically the 'fifth sweep' of that cohort study, conducted in 1992

PIAT   Peabody Individual Achievement Test; in this report, specifically the Reading Recognition subtest

PPVT   Peabody Picture Vocabulary Test; in this report, specifically Form L – Revised

s.d.   standard deviation

Statistical notes

1. In this report, whenever a result is said to be statistically significant, the statistical test employed showed the relevant mean scores, etc., to be significantly different at the 5 per cent level of confidence ($p<0.05$), or better.

2. 'Attrition' means the tendency for sample sizes to diminish over time as fewer people return for re-testing. Within that, 'differential attrition' means that those who do not return for re-testing are not representative of the whole of the original sample; for example, they may tend to have lower original scores.

3. 'Wash-out' means the tendency for the beneficial effect that an intervention has while it is operating to disappear after it ends. This would be shown in a tendency for average scores to fall back to the starting level when subjects are followed up some time after the initiative has ended.

The lead partners in the Demonstration Programmes were: South Glamorgan LEA, Norfolk County Council, North Tyneside Council and Liverpool Community College in partnership with the LEA. The range of partners included Adult Basic Skills services, LEAs, schools, colleges, TECs and libraries. The schools where the programmes were based were:

- Herbert Thompson Infants School, Ely, Cardiff
- Larkman First School, Norwich
- Shiremoor First School, North Tyneside
- Stockton Wood Infants School, Speke

Members of the evaluation team

Dr Greg Brooks, Senior Research Officer at NFER, Slough, was the Project Leader, carried out fieldwork in Norfolk, and was the principal author of this report.

Dr Tom Gorman, consultant to NFER, based in Worcestershire, carried out fieldwork in Cardiff, devised the marking systems for parents' and children's writing, marked all the scripts, and wrote the commentary on them.

John Harman, consultant to NFER, based in Berkshire, analysed the parent interviews and wrote the commentary on them.

Tim Self was the project statistician until February 1995.

Dougal Hutchison, Chief Statistician at NFER, was the project statistician from March 1995.

Anne Wilkin, Assistant Research Officer at NFER's Northern Office in York, carried out fieldwork in Liverpool and North Tyneside.

Acknowledgements

The authors wish to express their thanks to:

- our colleague, Dr Sandie Schagen, for reading and commenting on two drafts of this report
- Dr Peter Shepherd and Dr Kate Smith of City University, London, for providing training on the Peabody tests.
- Christopher Brooks, who marked most of the cloze tests and checked all the statistics in the text
- Annabel Hemstedt and her colleagues at the Basic Skills Agency, for constant support
- Graham Frater, Chairperson, and all the other members of the evaluation Steering Group, for much help and advice
- the Adult Basic Skills and Early Years Co-ordinators and other teachers in the Programmes, for stalwartly gathering most of the data for us
- their colleagues in the host schools and local partner bodies, for their help and collaboration

and especially to

- all the parents and children involved, for enduring so much testing, and for the inspiration their progress gave to everyone who saw it.

Executive Summary

The Family Literacy Demonstration Programmes

- The four Programmes were based in areas of multiple deprivation in Cardiff, Liverpool, Norfolk and North Tyneside.

- The courses lasted 96 hours over 12 weeks.

- They were provided for children aged 3 to 6 and their parents (96 per cent of participating parents were mothers).

- On entry, the parents had low levels of literacy, and many of their children were severely disadvantaged for learning by low development in vocabulary and in emergent reading and writing.

- Parents worked on their own literacy, built on home literacy activities and learned how to extend the help they gave their children.

- The children were given intensive early years teaching, with a strong emphasis on writing and talk as well as reading.

- In joint sessions, the parents worked with their children and used the strategies they had been taught for helping them.

Main Findings

The Basic Skills Agency's triple aims were to boost children's literacy, parents' ability to help their children, and parents' literacy; *overall, the aims were fulfilled in great detail.*

Benefits to the children

- The children made *greater-than-expected average improvements in vocabulary and reading during the courses and in the 12 weeks after them.*

- *In writing, they made substantial average improvements during the courses, and in the 12 weeks after them, and in the next six months.*

- Thus many of the children had benefited in *all three aspects of language.*

- Some of the specific *gains made by children were:*
  - the standardised mean score for *vocabulary rose from 85 to 93*
  - the proportion whose lack of vocabulary would leave them *struggling in school fell from 54 per cent to 31 per cent*
  - the proportion whose lack of vocabulary would leave them *severely disadvantaged for learning fell from 17 per cent to six per cent*
  - the standardised mean score for *reading rose from 84 to 92*
  - the proportion whose low reading level would leave them *struggling in school fell from 67 per cent to 35 per cent*
  - the proportion whose low reading level would leave them *severely disadvantaged for learning fell from 24 per cent to nine per cent*
  - during the courses, the proportion of school-age *children who had not yet made the crucial transition to writing words fell from 62 per cent to 43 per cent.*
- Therefore the initiative *was working for the great majority of children; a high proportion of them were better equipped for school learning.*

Boost to the parents' ability to help their children

- There were *substantial increases in literacy-related home activities,* and these became *firmly embedded* in family practice.
- Parents also reported *substantial increases in their ability to help their children* with language and literacy and in their *confidence* in doing so.
- Parents seemed to feel that *a barrier between school practice and home activities had been crossed.*
- Parents were beginning to *enjoy their own success as they saw their children's progress.*

Benefits to the parents

- *91 per cent of parents who started a course completed it and attendance rates were consistently high.*
- During the courses, *the parents improved their average reading test scores by five per cent* of the maximum score, *and their average writing score by 10 per cent* of the starting level.
- *95 per cent of all the parents attained partial or full accreditation of a level of Wordpower.*
- Over half (52 per cent) of the parents responding also referred to a *growth in their confidence,* and many reported other improvements in social skills.

- *The number of parents actively involved in their children's schools increased significantly.*
- At the end of the course, *over 80 per cent of parents planned to go on studying*, and *12 weeks after the courses 70 per cent were actually doing a further course.*

Bonus Effects

Not only were all the Agency's aims fulfilled, but the Programmes' achievements also extended *considerably beyond the stated targets*:

- The Programmes acted as *women's access courses.*
- All the gains made by parents and children during the course were *at least sustained* up to 9 months afterwards, and in many cases there were *further improvements.*
- *Communication* between parents and children *improved markedly.*
- Parents reported considerable improvement in their ability to *communicate with their children's teachers.*
- Through the extra courses set up during the lifetime of the evaluation, the Agency's *model was shown to be applicable* in different settings.

Human Factors in the Programmes' Success

The most important of these were:

- the clear *purpose* set by the Agency
- the careful *selection* of Programmes and teachers
- the *focusing* of everyone's minds on achieving a great deal in a fixed time
- detailed and collaborative *joint planning*
- the strong aspirations and motivation that *parents brought* to the Programmes
- the clear *picture* given to parents of *what they could achieve* for themselves and for their children
- the joint purpose and *group cohesion* achieved by parents
- the *excellent and reflective teaching*
- the massive boost given to the parents' *confidence*
- the genuinely intergenerational nature of the courses
- the *creative synthesis in the joint sessions*, with their immediate *feedback*, the sense of *achievement* they gave parents, and the *enjoyment and learning* they gave children.

Unit Cost and Value for Money

- The cost per participant-learning hour was £3.47.

- The evaluators judged that *the Family Literacy Programmes represented good value for money.*

Principal Judgements and Recommendations

- *The Basic Skills Agency's Family Literacy Demonstration Programmes initiative has achieved great success.*

- *The evaluators judged it to be one of the most effective initiatives they had ever encountered, and well worth building on.*

- *The Family Literacy initiative should therefore be continued and made available more widely across the country.*

Structure of this report

This is the final report on the evaluation by the National Foundation for Educational Research (NFER) of the Basic Skills Agency's Family Literacy Demonstration Programmes.

Those Programmes ran from October 1993 to December 1995, and the evaluation covered the period from April 1994 to October 1995.

This report covers and analyses all facets of the evaluation. Its first purpose is to describe the Family Literacy initiative, the Programmes and the evaluation, and this is done in chapters 1 to 4 and Appendix A.

The second, and major, purpose of this report is to answer three overall questions:

- How effective were the Family Literacy Demonstration Programmes?
- Why?
- What lessons and recommendations can be drawn?

The answers to these questions are given in chapters 5 to 8, 9 to 10, and 11 to 12, respectively.

CHAPTER ONE

The origin and aims of the Basic Skills Agency's Family Literacy initiative

1.1 Origin: the scale of need

About one-sixth of the adult population of Britain has problems with basic literacy skills (Ekinsmyth and Bynner, 1994; Brooks, Foxman and Gorman, 1995). There is also evidence that, where parents have literacy difficulties, their children are also likely to struggle with reading and writing, and therefore to underachieve educationally (ALBSU, 1993; Bynner and Steedman, 1995, especially pp.47-50). Programmes which are designed to work with parents and young children together could have a powerful impact not only on adults' skills, but also on children's attainment and therefore in helping to prevent the recurring intergenerational cycle of low attainment. St. Pierre *et al.* (1994) summarised research in the United States which supports this notion; Hannon (1995; Hannon *et al.*, 1990) traced the development and analysed the impact of programmes to involve parents in supporting the development of their children's literacy; Sylva and Hurry (1995) showed the importance for children's attainment of an early literacy-rich environment and parental encouragement; and Bynner and Steedman (1995) showed that in Britain pre-school educational experience had long-term effects on people's attainment.

During 1992-93 the Basic Skills Agency (then called ALBSU – the Adult Literacy and Basic Skills Unit) undertook development work on Family Literacy, to devise a model for an initiative which would have the greatest chance of successful impact in England and Wales. Dr Tom Sticht, a leading researcher on family literacy in the USA, and Professor Hazel Francis, the Institute of Education, acted as consultants to the Agency.

1.2 Aims: parents and children together

The term 'family literacy' itself appears to have been coined by Taylor (1983). Since then, as Nickse (1993; Nickse and Quezada, 1994) in the United States and Topping and Wolfendale (1995) in Britain have pointed out, the term has come to have a range of meanings:

- *home visits to encourage literacy-related activities in the home*

1

- *school- or community-based programmes which seek to encourage parental involvement in reading in order to benefit their children*

- *programmes intended to improve the skills of parents with low levels of literacy*

- *school-based supplementary reading programmes for children*

- *intergenerational programmes, that is, ones in which both parents and children receive teaching.*

All of these can be considered 'family literacy' in a broad sense, since they all imply working with low-literacy families with the intention of boosting parents' and/or children's attainment. But only the last of the types of programme just listed is fully 'intergenerational', in the sense of aiming to improve the skills of both parents and children, and providing tuition for both for that purpose. This is the sense in which the term 'intergenerational' will be used in this report. It is therefore more precise than the sense in which it is used by, for example, Paratore (1995), who uses it to describe programmes in which parents are the focus of teaching, although the intention is that, through them, children will be the main beneficiaries.

In the more precise sense intended here, intergenerational Family Literacy initiatives not only involve (at least) two generations in the family, but have also been described as 'three-pronged', in that they have the triple aim of

- *improving parents' own literacy skills*

- *improving parents' ability to help their children with the early stages of learning to read and write*

- *boosting young children's acquisition of reading and writing.*

The Basic Skills Agency's Family Literacy initiative in England and Wales was designed from the start to be intergenerational in this 'two-generation, three-pronged' sense. A recent review by Topping and Wolfendale (1995) appears to show that there have been no previous initiatives of exactly this type in Britain. It was therefore also intended to be complementary to other initiatives, not to replace them. However, it was hoped that it would be at least as effective as other forms of provision; St. Pierre *et al.* (1994) also summarised research in the United States which suggested that parent-only and home-visiting programmes were relatively ineffective in boosting children's attainment.

CHAPTER TWO

Background, aims and objectives of the Family Literacy initiative

This chapter first gives the background to the Basic Skills Agency's Family Literacy initiative, and then states the principal requirements (aims and objectives) which the Agency set for its four Family Literacy Demonstration Programmes.

2.1 Background to the initiative

With funding from the (then) Department for Education and the Welsh Office, the Basic Skills Agency established the Family Literacy initiative in October 1993. Two of its overall aims were:

- *to raise standards of literacy among adults with difficulties and their children, and*

- *to extend awareness of the importance of literacy and the role of family literacy.*

The initiative was complementary to initiatives being mounted by other providers, and multi-faceted. It comprised a Small Grants programme, a small number of Demonstration Programmes, major promotional work with the BBC, and the production of training and support materials for teachers. Under the Small Grants programme, the Agency gave amounts ranging from a few hundred pounds up to a maximum of £5,000 to small-scale, local initiatives which could show both a family literacy aspect and at least equivalent funding from local sources.

The Demonstration Programmes were on a much larger scale. When they were set up, they were intended to run for two years (later extended by a term), and were to have their own premises (at least at their main site) and appropriate numbers of specialist staff. Whereas the Small Grants went to initiatives which had to meet only a few criteria to qualify, the Demonstration Programmes were designed to act as the 'test bed' for an intensive trial of a detailed model with highly specific aims (see next section), and to demonstrate the possibilities and value of that model, in order to underpin the case for subsequent substantial development. While 25 per cent of the Programmes' funding was provided by local partners, the majority came through the Agency.

The four Demonstration Programmes which are the subject of this evaluation were set up in areas of multiple deprivation in Cardiff, Liverpool, Norfolk and North Tyneside.

Originally, five Demonstration Programmes were established. For local reasons beyond the Agency's control, one ceased to operate after two terms of teaching, and was not covered by this evaluation. That Programme had by design been set up in an area where many of the target parents were bilingual and members of ethnic minorities, and its cessation meant that those parts of the target population were not as fully represented in the evaluation as had been intended. Targeting of those groups was, however, pursued through the Small Grants programme.

2.2 The Agency's requirements on the Programmes

The overall aims set by the Agency for the Programmes were the three stated at the end of chapter 1: to boost parents' own literacy, their ability to help their children, and their children's literacy.

The approach by which the Agency intended the Programmes to achieve those aims was set out in a precise model embodying specific prerequisites and objectives. The prerequisites included:

- *working in partnership with a range of organisations*

- *locating the Programmes in areas of multiple deprivation*

- *meeting specified site requirements*

- *providing local funding, and a commitment to continuation through convincing local partners of the value of the Programmes*

- *providing a crèche for younger children at every site, and help with transport for families who needed it*

- *meeting the Agency's Quality Standards, which include an appropriate student/teacher ratio, and staff with appropriate, nationally recognised qualifications incorporating both Adult Basic Skills and Early Years teachers, and advice and guidance on progression*

- *targeting parents who performed at or below Level 1 of the Agency's Communication Skills Standards. Particular priority was to be given to people performing at or below Foundation Level of the Standards, and it was envisaged that at least 30 per cent of participants would be from this group*

- *running free 12-week courses for up to 12 parents and their children*

- *providing parents with six hours of accredited basic skills instruction per week*

- *providing children with six hours of language and literacy development per week*

- *providing parents and children with two hours per week of joint sessions on supporting early language and literacy.*

There was also one prerequisite on parents, namely that, to be eligible to attend, each parent had to have at least one child aged between 3 years 0 months (3:00) and 6 years 11 months (6:11) at the beginning of the course, and both parent and child had to attend.

The objectives in terms of outcomes included the following:

- *involvement, over the first five terms of teaching, of approximately 150 parents and 180 children*

- *improvement in the literacy of 80 per cent of parents*

- *improvement in the early literacy skills of 80 per cent of children*

- *achievement of accreditation by 70 per cent of parents*

- *improved knowledge of methods of fostering early literacy by 80 per cent of parents*

- *a retention rate of 75 per cent of families for the 12-week period of the courses.*

Thus the model was very precise, detailed and demanding.

It also differed in four significant ways from many existing programmes.

First, it differed sharply from both family literacy programmes in the United States and typical Adult Basic Skills provision in this country in having a fixed amount of time, 96 hours in all. Many programmes, here and in the US, operate on a drop in or open learning model, such that students may drop and resume their involvement as they wish, and pressure to achieve accreditation within a certain time is absent (for recent British evidence on this, see Kambouri and Francis, 1994). This makes the provision of a structured programme difficult, for both teachers and students. Despite this, local partners in one of the Demonstration Programme areas initially expressed scepticism that the Agency's intensive model would work. However, the Family Literacy Demonstration Programmes were deliberately intended to show what could be achieved within a reasonable but clearly defined time limit.

Another feature which set this model apart from some US programmes was that all participating parents were to be volunteers. In some US programmes participation in adult literacy or (broadly defined) family literacy courses is linked to social security benefits. This was ruled out in the Agency's model. There was not even to be any element of 'referral' from social services or other agencies, in order to avoid the imputation of deficiency, the consequent attachment of stigma, and the risk of undermining the motivation of participating parents.

Again, many US programmes set much wider aims than the educational ones defined here. For instance, they may have social and/or socioeconomic objectives, including aspirations for the participating parents' employment status and income level. Such wide aims were not the primary focus of the Agency's model, which focused precisely and clearly on the parents' and children's language and literacy.

On the other hand, within their educational aims, as Dickinson (1994) pointed out, many parental involvement, emergent literacy and family literacy schemes in the United States stress reading above all, and this is also true in Britain. Because the Agency agreed that 'literacy is more than book reading' (Barton, 1995, p.3), the Family Literacy initiative incorporated reading, writing and talking from the outset.

The most important feature of the model, however, was its truly **intergenerational** nature. This was embodied in particular in the triple aims and in the parallel and joint sessions, and constituted the most distinctive aspect of the Programmes.

CHAPTER THREE

Description of the Family Literacy Demonstration Programmes

———

This chapter first outlines the timetables of the four Family Literacy Demonstration Programmes. The bulk of the chapter consists of a description of the Programmes, covering the parents', children's and joint sessions.

3.1 An outline of the Demonstration Programmes

Of the four continuing Demonstration Programmes, three were set up in October 1993 and began teaching in January 1994, while the fourth was set up in January 1994 and began teaching in April 1994. Programme staff received detailed training from the Agency at residential sessions in London. Each Programme ran at least two courses each term. All began with courses only at their main site. Thereafter, most Programmes ran at least one course at their main site each term while also running at least one elsewhere; sites other than the main ones tended to be used intermittently. Though this was not an explicit requirement, each Programme had its main site, and almost all of its other sites, based in or very close to an infant or primary school.

In their separate sessions, the parents worked on their own literacy (and numeracy) skills and towards accreditation for their literacy achievements. They also learnt about the early stages of literacy, and how they could help their children achieve them successfully. The children-only sessions were a blend of nursery and infant school practices and approaches, as appropriate to the ages of the particular children attending. In the joint sessions, the parents worked with their own children and applied what they had learnt in the separate sessions about helping them.

The structure of the courses is illustrated by the two course timetables reproduced on the following pages. The timetables are from different Programmes, and from different terms.

Timetable – Programme A

Joint Activity	Outcome for parents	Outcome for children
Creative Play Show parents a range of art/craft activities:- painting, drawing, modelling, collage, junk modelling.	Show parents the value of creative activities. Show the importance of encouragement and praise. Show them that it is cheap and easy to do these things at home.	Encourage children to experiment. Give them the opportunity to use tools and materials to develop hand control. Develop a wide range of language skills.
Toy Library and Toys Discuss toys with parents. Difference between home and school toys. Tell stories using puppets. Talk about puppets. Make a puppet. Choose a toy for home.	Understand the importance of imagination and role play. Share a story telling and puppet making session with the children. Be comfortable borrowing books and toys.	Develop listening skills for stories. Talk about animals, animal noises and characters. Develop imagination and confidence. Develop practical skills for making puppets. Learn to take care of borrowed toys.
Games Parents look at a range of games available for home use and for school. Parents and children to choose from a range of games to play together.	Show how individual games can teach specific skills. Learn how they are used in school. Show parents how much they help their children by playing games at home.	Share games with parents. Learn social skills, e.g. turns, winning/losing. Learn skills e.g. memory, colour, shape, numbers.
Early Reading Walk with parents and children near to school. Look for signs, symbols, road names etc. Buy fruit with a shopping list. Taste fruits and talk about them. Record likes and dislikes. Read story of *The Avocado Baby*.	Show parents importance of environmental print. Help them to set an example for reading and writing (list). Help them to see the opportunities in everyday activities for learning new language.	Learn to be more aware of print around them. Learn to compare print on map/list with what they see. Concentrate on what they are looking for. Learn names of fruits and language to describe the tastes and textures. Learn to record their findings on a chart. Listen to instructions and to a story.

Joint Activity	Outcome for parents	Outcome for children
Looking at books Visit the library with the children. Listen to a talk by the librarian. Look at a range of books and tapes. Listen to stories being read by the librarian. Read stories to the children.	Become more aware of the range of books and tapes available for children. Help them to see the opportunities for learning and for pleasure to be had from books. Share books with their children. Become more aware of equal opportunities. Join the library if they want to.	Develop listening skills while they have stories. Become more confident in contributing to stories e.g. prediction skills, re-telling stories, what happens next. Share books with their parents. Become familiar with the library. Take books home to continue reading.
Writing and drawing Show parents a range of activities and materials to encourage writing skills e.g. felts, crayons, cutting, paperplay, chalks, pastels, paints, stories, rhymes. Practise these with the children.	Help parents recognise the importance of stages in children's drawing and writing. Become confident that they can provide these opportunities at home. Help them to value things they do at home e.g. writing lists, cards, paper planes, buying colouring books etc.	Practise forming letters and drawing with a variety of materials. Learning to write as part of everyday role playing games. Gaining more hand control from cutting, colouring, etc. Sharing activities with parents.
Science Lay out a choice of activities for children to try. Explain the language (scientific and everyday) which children learn from the activities.	Become more confident that everyday activities help children learn science and literacy skills e.g. cooking, floating and sinking, growing things, electricity. Become less afraid that 'science' is something they will not understand. Help them understand the National Curriculum.	Give children the chance to investigate. Help them to predict what they think will happen. Help them to observe carefully and explain what they see. Learn new language e.g. melt, dissolve, float. Help them to record what they are doing or have found out.
The Language of Maths		
Day Out Discuss the possibilities for a day out. Discuss what children might get from it. e.g. do they need a booklet/list? Plan travel and other details.	Realise that outings can be fun without being extravagant. Realise that children benefit from excitement and new experiences of all kinds. Share a fun day with their children and other parents.	Share a day out with their parents. Learn to concentrate and look out for things while they are travelling. Talk about the experience. Use the day out as inspiration for drawing, writing and talking long after the event.

Timetable – Programme B

Week	ADULT	JOINT
1	NFER Assessment ***Making games*** Parents to make a game for their child – thinking about literacy skills involved when playing it. Introduction to computers.	***Environmental Print*** ***The importance of games*** Bought and home-made games Examples of print seen in shops etc. Talk by Early Years Worker.
2	NFER Assessment ***Completing and making games*** Parents to evaluate the games and analyse the skills needed to play them. Using the computers to type up instructions for games.	***The importance of play*** Guest Speaker: a Nursery Teacher Parents to watch a video on play – discuss and then play a variety of games which encourage the development of early literacy skills with their child.
3	***Spelling*** Discussion on why we need to spell Spelling methods and rules Using a Dictionary – Practical Exercises linked to both adults and children. Examples of home-made spelling games. (This session requested by parents)	***Story Telling*** Guest Speaker: a member of the Young People's Library Service Making flap books and pop up cards Reading books especially those associated with farm animals.
4	***Making the Jolly Postman Books*** Informal letters re above then group discussion on how to make the book and what to include Using computers to produce the book.	***Reading with your child*** Guest Speaker: a Reception Teacher Making an "All About Me" book, nursery rhymes associated with animals. Following instructions to make a hat or house. Making finger puppets of animals.
5	Continuing with *Jolly Postman book* Using computers and computer graphics.	***Writing Skills*** Talk by Early Years Worker on how to encourage writing skills at home. Zig zag books with the child's name in, sequencing pictures to make own story book, writing name using play dough.
6	***Visit Farm*** Parents to organise outing and help their children to complete the activity books supplied and extend the language skills of their child.	Tour of the farm: lots of language opportunity about animals, their sounds, parts of the body and where the animals live etc. To complete an activity booklet which the children took to the farm.

Week	ADULT	JOINT
7	***Completing the parent's book*** Visit to local Central Library; using the various reference systems, joining the library etc. (All of these activities are linked to Wordpower *)	***Recording the visit*** Each child produces a page to go into a joint book on what we did at the Farm. Make various animals for a wall frieze to decorate the room.
8	***Diet*** Guest Speaker: a dietician – video on healthy eating, quiz, group discussion, worksheets and putting together a recipe book for the children using the computers.	***Using newspapers to promote literacy and numeracy*** Guest speaker from the local evening paper. Each child is given a booklet with lots of cut and stick activities.
9	***Communication*** Verbal, non-verbal and written communication linked to Wordpower and the use of the computers. (Emphasis on decoding)	***Listening Skills*** Guest Speaker: a police constable to talk on Stranger Danger. Sound shakers, sound lotto, learning name and address using labels and doors, listening to a tape, answering questions.
10	***Assessment Books*** Thinking about skills the children have or need to acquire and then putting together an interactive book of activities which will encourage these skills in their child.	***T.V., Videos and Computers*** How to use the above as educational tools. Talk from the Early Years Worker. Lots of hands on experience of education software etc.
11	***Assessment Books*** continued Using the computer and more group discussion on what can be included in the books. Discussion on activities for next week's joint session.	***Activities Sessions*** Parents to provide a series of activities for the children e.g. decorating biscuits, making kites, face mask etc.
12	***Advice and Guidance*** Guest speakers from local advice organisations and FE College – where to next? NFER Assessment.	***Free Party*** at local burger bar to celebrate the end of the course. This will also include the children colouring in posters and worksheets.
13	Parents welcome to complete any work necessary for certification.	

*Wordpower is the City and Guilds' competence-based accreditation system designed to certificate achievement in communication skills, from beginner level through increasing levels of difficulty.

A more detailed picture of the content and teaching approaches of the Programmes is given in the remaining sections of this chapter, which deal in turn with the parents' sessions, the children's sessions, and the joint sessions.

3.2 The range of activities in parents' sessions

In the 18 parents' sessions observed, the content almost always had a dual purpose:

> • *to improve the parents' literacy (and in so doing build towards accreditation within Wordpower), and*

> • *to prepare for or practise a language- or literacy-related activity which could be used with children (and, typically, one of the activities which the children were given in their parallel session was intended to mesh with this).*

For example, two sessions were observed in which parents wrote about and discussed their 'Holiday of a Lifetime'. For Wordpower purposes, this involved using timetables and maps, and both aspects earned credit. The topic was also one which could lead to animated discussion and activities with children. In the Early Years room, amongst other activities that morning, the children had been read a story involving three wishes, and had talked and, where possible, written about their own three wishes. A joint session of the sort to which this could lead is described in section 3.8 below.

The topics of some of the other parents' sessions observed were as follows:

> • *imperial to metric conversion*

> • *studying communication systems other than English (e.g. signing, other alphabets, international road signs) as illustrations of how difficult learning to read is*

> • *formal and informal language*

> • *forms and completing them*

> • *writing letters*

> • *spelling*

> • *making books*

> • *children's early reading and writing*

> • *preparing for joint cooking with children*

> • *preparing for joint session on handwriting.*

Thus most sessions were explicitly on language, and the rest laid stress on the communicative aspects of the topic. This enabled parents to develop all aspects of their support for children's language and literacy, as in the ORIM (Opportunities – Recognition – Interaction – Modelling) approach outlined by Hannon (1995, p.51).

The teachers of course provided the input to most sessions, but all the Programmes also brought in outsiders for specific purposes, for example:

- *First Aiders to give training*

- *puppet-makers to demonstrate both making and using puppets*

- *an Adult Basic Skills colleague to describe further courses*

- *a primary headteacher to talk about the development of writing*

- *an LEA adviser talking about national curriculum science, and demonstrating some experiments to try out with children*

- *a dietician exploring questions of healthy eating*

- *a health worker giving a session on drugs.*

3.3 Teaching approaches in parents' sessions

The teaching approaches in the parents' sessions were a balanced blend of whole-group, small group and individual. Sessions would typically begin with a whole-group phase, often including completion and/or evaluation of the previous session's work, and always including the teacher's description and justification of what was intended for that session.

Often this evoked reflections and comments from the students, and teachers exercised tact in bringing the discussion back on track. When the topic had been introduced and the practical activities were begun, information sheets and worksheets were much in evidence, and small group or individual working (some of it on a word-processor) was the norm. It was observed that, at this stage, the teachers were often to be found alongside the students who needed their help most when that help was needed, though without making it seem that those students had particular deficiencies. Many sessions ended with a further brief whole-group phase, tackling questions arising, suggesting home-work and leading to joint sessions.

3.4 An example of an effective session for parents

A summary of one of the parents' sessions observed is given in Box 1.

Box 1: An effective parents' session

In the morning, a dietician had visited to talk about and analyse foods. In this afternoon session beginning at 13.25, the Adult Basic Skills teacher first asked each of the five parents present in turn what they let their children do in the kitchen, and wrote their answers on the flip chart. She commented that what they were doing was giving their children a good grounding for literacy and numeracy. When she asked what skills the children were using, the parents answered 'Coordination' and 'Quantities'.

The teacher then talked about the sort of language they could use in these situations: 'greater than', 'more/less than', 'runny', 'smooth'. The question 'What about adding the ingredients, what else can you let them do?' elicited 'Measuring', and 'What about when you're making sandwiches?' the answer 'Quarters' – 'Yes, fractions, lovely'.

After some further questions along these lines, at 13.40 the teacher asked the parents to write out the recipes they had brought along; the copies were to go into a booklet similar to one on the wall labelled Delicious Meals for Children made by parents on a previous course. The teacher reminded parents who were going to put their recipes on the word-processor that they would need three copies, one each for their word-processing pack, their own file and to put in the book. While the parents copied out their recipes, amid discussion about various supermarkets, the teacher moved around encouraging them.

By 13.55 the first parent was ready to start typing up on one of the word-processors; others soon followed, one using a lap-top. At 14.00 the teacher told the parents who were still writing to think about the fine motor skills the children would be using when cooking, and the language, for example what the mixture looks like, what it feels like. When she read through some of the finished recipes, she commented, 'Yes, that's excellent, it's got all the good things in.'

By 14.15 all the parents had finished writing, but no more word-processors were available. The teacher asked, 'Do you want some Wordpower to do while you're waiting?' She then went through with each parent what they still needed to do to complete the accreditation they were aiming at, and showed them the books where they would find it. The session continued in this way, with parents moving between the word-processors and Wordpower, until 15.15.

This session displayed exactly the blending of aims that was the major feature of the parents' sessions: they worked on their own literacy, and on the accreditation that would recognise that, and prepared to use the content in the ensuing joint session. Embedded within the content was attention to healthy eating, to numeracy to a minor extent, and above all to children's language and motor development. The teaching approach moved smoothly and appropriately from whole-group to individual. And the teacher was both constantly encouraging and constantly enabling parents to move their own skills and insights on.

3.5 The range of activities and teaching approaches in children's sessions

In each of the 19 children's sessions that were observed, a range of activities was provided to fill the time both enjoyably and profitably. Just one session was led by a visitor, a local railway official who had come to talk about safety; all the other sessions observed were led by teachers. Often a session both began and ended with the teacher reading a story to the children. They would often be invited to join in the telling, and in the singing of nursery rhymes and other songs. Much of the central part of the sessions would be spent in individual or very small group activities: using building blocks, painting, playing house, imaginative play with dolls and other toys, taking turns on a computer, drawing, writing. The Early Years rooms were set up with designated areas for these activities. The Early Years teacher and nursery assistant would migrate between children, providing assistance and, where necessary, discipline, and seeking always to extend children's imagination and vocabulary.

Some of the more distinctive activities included growing cress, making masks, drawing items from a 'Feelie bag' to trigger nursery rhymes, cutting out mobiles or pieces for a collage, making a chart of food likes and dislikes, finger-painting, interpreting sound tapes and other listening activities, collecting words for personal 'banks', 'jars' or 'toolkits', and writing letters to their parents. There was a great deal of work on colour words, and on words for size and quantity relationships and for degrees of similarity. **Embedded everywhere was attention to the development of fine motor control, language and imagination. The teachers were always alert to children's attention spans, to their individual language development needs, and to the need to balance a menu of activities and individual progression with spontaneity and the children's right to choose.** Not all sessions could hope for the serendipity of one where children were cutting out *'Incy Wincy Spider'* mobiles and found a real spider in the sink.

Of the 19 children's sessions observed, only one seemed to the fieldworker to be less effective than it could have been. The teacher, though highly experienced in primary schools, was relatively new to Early Years, and it may be that previous experience at this age-level is a prerequisite for immediate effectiveness in Family Literacy.

3.6 An example of an effective session for children

Certainly, when the same teacher was later observed leading another children's session, that session was much more effective, and typical of those seen. This session is described in Box 2.

Box 2: An effective children's session

While the teacher and her assistant got various items ready, two children came to talk to the fieldworker at the writers' table, wrote their names for him, asked his, and drew. Having gathered the children in the Story corner, the teacher introduced the Feelie Bag game, each child drawing an item and the group singing an appropriate song. The teacher tape-recorded some children saying their rhymes after the singing. All eight children in the group had a turn, so that this activity lasted 19 minutes.

Next, the main activity was to be painting 'branches' for a cardboard tree, on which rhymes were to be hung the following day. The teacher helped some children don waterproofs for this, while the assistant played 'magnetic fishing' with most of the rest, and two played with a toy farm. Soon, two children switched to the 'hammering blocks into a board' table, while two others, at the fieldworker's table, drew round their hands and cut out the shapes, concentrating hard on the task.

Twenty minutes after the first children had put on waterproofs, another child did so, and joined the group working steadily at their painting. Two others were now at the plasticine table; the assistant joined them and gave their activity more focus. Soon after this, painting ceased, so the assistant talked to that group about colours, while playing a memory card game with them.

The teacher had now been supervising four children at magnetic fishing for 15 minutes, and kept this going for some minutes more. When they wanted to, children from each of these groups peeled off and joined in with plasticine. Two others left fishing for the central table and were joined by a third. Soon after this, the teacher was still at fishing with one boy, one boy was at the central table, one was at the fieldworker's table, two children were with the assistant in the story corner, and three were playing with plasticine. The teacher moved to this last group; the assistant and two children began singing *'Baa Baa Black Sheep'* and were joined by a third.

An hour and 10 minutes from the start of the session, with 20 minutes to go, the teacher announced that tidying up would soon begin. This went on through the singing of the *'The Wheels on the Bus'* and *'I Hear Thunder'*, and the playing of *'The Baker's Shop'* on tape.

With 10 minutes to go, the teacher called all the children to sit in a circle. The teacher and some children counted out the pennies needed for *'The Baker's Shop'*, then the teacher counted out the (real) buns to be used (and eaten). A girl was appointed baker and all sang, counting downwards each time and paying a penny for a bun. Once every child had a bun and the buns were eaten, the teacher asked the 'baker' to count how much money she had made today. The session ended when the seven mothers and one father arrived to collect their children.

Throughout the session described in Box 2, both teachers had kept the children's interest and attention going, while allowing children to switch activities when they wished, had directed purposeful uses of language (in talk, reading and writing) and been very clear about what those and the other objectives were, and had always been where they were most needed. The considerable range of ages in the group had been handled adroitly. **The overall impression was of a thoroughly useful session, an imaginative, creative and language-developing kaleidoscope.** So were all but one of the children's sessions observed.

3.7 The range of activities and teaching approaches in joint sessions

The activities in the 17 joint sessions observed included:

- *sequencing pictures to make a story*
- *meeting a snake*
- *testing which materials would complete an electrical circuit on a picture of a lighthouse*
- *visiting a former lighthouse*
- *puppet-making*
- *making a calendar and weather chart*
- *library visits*
- *listening and speaking activities, e.g. sound lotto*
- *science experiments and writing up the results*
- *a shopping walk*
- *cooking*
- *blindfold tasting of foods to encourage more precise description.*

In addition to joint sessions 'on site', each course group had an outing, and the range of those was also wide: a zoo, a former lighthouse, etc. The purpose was always dual: to have fun, but also to demonstrate to parents that trips could be made deliberately educational while not detracting from the enjoyment but actually enhancing it.

Two of the joint sessions observed had a single 'presenter': in one, a parent had brought along a live snake for the children and other parents to learn about, and in the other a police officer talked about Stranger Danger. Otherwise, almost all joint sessions involved parents and children working together. In these sessions, Adult Basic Skills and Early Years teachers did do some teaching, often unobtrusively; but most of the teaching was done by the parents.

The allocation of the teaching role depended on the activity. A two-part joint session was observed in one Programme in which the first part was a shopping walk. The Early Years teacher had earlier explained to the parents what was planned, and now led the walk, choosing particular children to go into certain shops to select and try small quantities of various foodstuffs. She thus modelled for the parents how to make educational, especially language development, capital out of this seemingly obvious, but neglected, everyday opportunity. Back at the course site, the parents took over as the foodstuffs just bought became ingredients in a joint cooking session.

In all but two of the 'small-group' joint sessions observed, when joint activities began, the parents worked very enthusiastically and purposefully with their children. They generally worked with their own children, though in one session a good deal of swapping was observed. In one of the two exceptional sessions, the Early Years Coordinator took charge of the language games being played; the parents seemed reluctant to join in and left things to her. She explained afterwards that the group had not gelled. In the remaining session, a visiting speaker had not brought promised activities and had used much less time than had been arranged, so that the teachers had to bring forward items intended for the following week. Despite their best efforts, the session had a 'patchwork' feel. Perhaps sensing this, some parents did not join in a singing game, and many let their children operate on their own. There may also have been some tension among the parents. However, in both cases the children would have got something out of the session. And all the other sessions were very effective.

3.8 An example of an effective joint session

The heights of effectiveness the joint sessions could reach can be illustrated by the 'Holiday of a Lifetime' session observed, and this is described in Box 3.

Box 3: An effective joint session

Nine parents and 10 children were involved, as well as three teachers. The parents had decided that morning that their 'Holiday of a Lifetime' would be a boat cruise somewhere abroad, involving a flight to begin with. Based on this, the children had decided (at 11.15, with the joint session beginning at 13.00) on what the precise activities would be, including passport control, the aeroplane in a corner of their room, the hotel in the rest of it, the boat outside, a shop and a travel agency.

By 13.10, when the fieldworker arrived, preparations were under way – the plane was being set up, passports were being made and stamped at passport control, etc. – a purposeful and language-rich frenzy, with all the parents and children busy and involved.

By the time 'take-off' approached (45 minutes later), many of the children had dressed up, and then a safety drill was held. After a one-minute flight and safe landing, everyone checked in to the hotel. The luggage consisted of small carrier bags printed with the name of the Programme. A mother here commented of her daughter, 'She's really getting into it.' The children soon solved the problem that the 'boat' (carpet) was too small: they tugged another out of doors. One girl wanted to take her shoes off (in a tarmac yard) because she was on a beach. With everyone in the boats, the Adult Basic Skills Coordinator asked the children if they could see fish over the side, and a mother told a child who had jumped over the side that she had just drowned. Then the ship's bell rang and it was time for refreshments.

Throughout the activity described in Box 3, there was purposeful fun, fantasy had full rein, and all the people (and furniture) were pressed into its service. Also, the teachers were continually asking the sort of questions that develop imagination and vocabulary.

CHAPTER FOUR

Outline of the evaluation

The first section of this chapter states the rationale for the commissioning of the evaluation, and the rest of the chapter gives a brief description of how it was carried out. A full description is given in Appendix A.

4.1 Rationale

It was important for the the Basic Skills Agency and its funders to know how successful the Family Literacy approach was. Gathering only subjective impressions, though necessary to understand how any gains were achieved, would not have been sufficient to convince funders that the aims had been met. The Agency therefore required the Programmes to gather detailed quantitative evidence on the parents' and children's starting points, and on the progress they made. But however impressive that evidence might be, it would be internal to the initiative, and might therefore be considered as telling only the story believed by those already committed to the initiative. All the interested parties needed to have evidence gathered and analysed by an organisation independent of the funders, the Agency and the Programmes.

In choosing to commission an independent evaluation, the Agency had rather few precedents in the family literacy field, and none in Britain of the three strand model. St Pierre *et al.* (1994) showed that, among the multiplicity of family literacy initiatives, in the broad sense, in the US, and even among the still quite large number of intergenerational initiatives there, just seven had been the subject of rigorous, quantitative, independent evaluation.

The Agency commissioned this independent evaluation of all four Demonstration Programmes from the National Foundation for Educational Research (NFER) in December 1993. The evaluation ran from January 1994 to December 1995. After a term's development work, it evaluated the Programmes' work in the four terms from summer 1994 to summer 1995 inclusive. Thus for three of the Programmes the evaluation began with the second teaching term and ended with the fifth, while for the remaining one it began with the first teaching term and ended with the fourth.

The evaluation looked at the effectiveness of the Programmes in achieving their triple aims. Besides evidence of those changes in literacy, the research focused on the **processes** by which the aims were achieved.

4.2 Forms of information

Evidence of gain from the Programmes might have emerged in:

- *parents and children*

- *performance in and attitudes towards literacy*

- *activities in the programme, at home and at school*

- *the short or the longer term.*

The evaluation was designed to gather appropriate quantitative and qualitative information on all these aspects.

Specifically, the forms of evidence collected by NFER were:

Quantitative data

on parents:
- background information
- reading attainment
- writing attainment
- literacy activities undertaken at home with children

on children:
- background information
- vocabulary development
- early reading development
- early writing development

Qualitative data

- interviews with parents
- interviews with Programme Coordinators
- observations of teaching sessions
- teachers' impressions.

In addition, the Programme Coordinators supplied NFER with a great deal of other relevant information and documentation.

4.3 Frequency of data collection

Quantitative data

Background information on parents and children was gathered once, near the beginning of the course. All the other forms of quantitative data were gathered at the beginning and end of the course for each of the four terms' cohorts of participants. Also, where possible within the timescale of the evaluation, quantitative data were collected 12 weeks and nine months after the end of the course. All quantitative data were gathered on NFER's behalf by Programme staff.

Qualitative data

Interviews with parents took place towards the end of each course, and on each of the follow-up occasions. Interviews with coordinators and observations of teaching sessions took place each term. Teachers' impressions were gathered in the spring and summer terms of 1995 only, on a limited number of children who moved from the Programmes into primary school.

4.4 Quantitative data-collection instruments

Background information on parents and children was collected through Adult and Child Profiles respectively.

To provide an estimate of their reading attainment, parents were asked on each occasion to complete a three-part cloze (gap-completion) test. To provide an estimate of their writing attainment, parents were asked on each occasion to answer three questions in writing.

Information on children's vocabulary, reading and writing was gathered for NFER by the Early Years Coordinators. For 'writing', they asked the children to produce:

- *a few lines or a sentence if they could*
- *if not, then their own name and some other letters*
- *if not that then letter-like forms or scribbles*
- *if not that then a copy of a few words*
- *and if not that then a drawing.*

For vocabulary and reading, the tests used were respectively the *Peabody Picture Vocabulary Test – Revised, Form L,* and the *Reading Recognition subtest* of the

Peabody Individual Achievement Tests. These tests are referred to in this report as the PPVT and PIAT respectively, and jointly as the 'Peabody tests'. They were both used in the National Child Development Study (NCDS) in 1992, and the data collected then provided 'control group' data for the children in this evaluation.

In order to investigate whether children's attainment has improved, it is necessary to test them. But the type of test is crucial. It is not enough to test before an intervention, re-test after it and show a gain, since that would be expected simply from the passage of time, from the fact that the children are growing and learning. What is needed is a demonstration that the improvement **is significantly greater than would be expected simply because the children are older by the time of the post-test.** The Peabody data from NCDS provided the necessary quantitative check on the attainment of the children in this study.

Information on literacy-related home activities was gathered indirectly. The main approach was to ask parents on each occasion of testing to estimate, in an interview with their tutor during which a relevant questionnaire was completed, how often they carried out certain literacy-related activities with their children at home (see Appendix B for the questionnaire and the data it yielded).

4.5 Qualitative data collection

Interviews with parents during the courses, interviews with Programme Coordinators (both Adult Basic Skills and Early Years) and observations of teaching sessions were all carried out by NFER researchers. Follow-up interviews with parents after the course were conducted by the Programmes' Adult Basic Skills Coordinators. All interviews were based on semi-structured interview schedules, and there was a separate schedule for the observations.

To gather teachers' impressions, each Early Years Coordinator was asked to speak to an Infant Teacher in her Programme's 'host' school, to identify with her one or two children who would be moving into that school from the Programme, and to ask the teacher to make a few observations on those children during one term and complete a brief questionnaire about them at the end of the term.

The qualitative data (including the Programme documents supplied to the evaluation team) were intended to help illuminate the processes by which any changes measured in the quantitative data were achieved.

CHAPTER FIVE

Starting points – the parents and children at the beginning of the courses

5.1 The parents and children: general characteristics

Between them, the four Programmes returned 361 parent profiles and 392 child profiles in the four terms of the evaluation. No parent had more than two participating children. Many parents had other children, but data were not systematically collected on them.

All but 30 parents and 30 children were of white European ethnicity, and all but 7 parents and 10 children were monolingual native speakers of English. Because the numbers of bilingual people and of people from ethnic minorities were small, neither ethnicity nor bilingualism was used as a reporting variable.

The parents were representative of the majority of the Agency's target group, even though so few bilingual people and members of ethnic minorities were recruited.

Gender

All but 14 (four per cent) of the parents were mothers, reflecting the still predominant pattern of child-rearing. Of the children, 198 were girls and 194 were boys.

Ages

The age-distribution of the parents is shown in Figure 5.1.

The age-distribution of the children for whom profiles were returned was as shown in Figure 5.2.

Figure 5.1: **Age-distribution of participating parents at start of course**

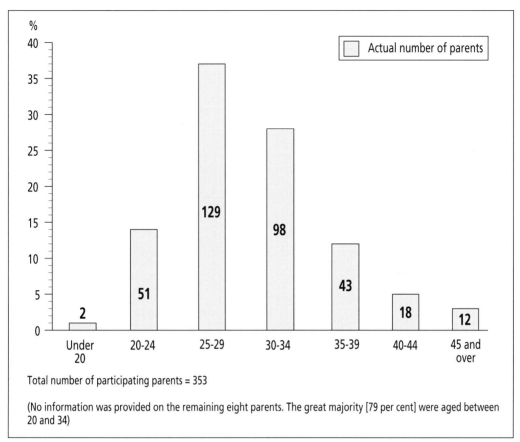

Total number of participating parents = 353

(No information was provided on the remaining eight parents. The great majority [79 per cent] were aged between 20 and 34)

Figure 5.2: **Age-distribution of participating children at start of course**

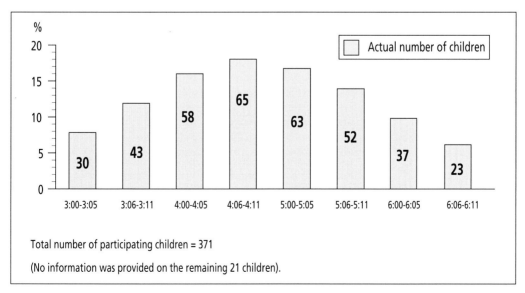

Total number of participating children = 371

(No information was provided on the remaining 21 children).

Parents' occupations

Participating parents were asked to classify their current occupation in one of nine categories. The categories, and the distribution of responses, were as shown in Figure 5.3, which also shows the percentage distribution in the NCDS cohort for comparison.

Figure 5.3: **Parents' occupations**

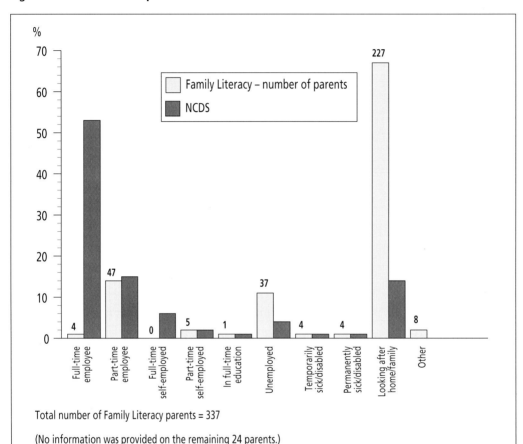

The few full-time employees in the Family Literacy sample were all shiftworkers. By far the most significant differences between the two samples were the much larger proportion of full-time employees, and the much smaller proportion of those looking after home/family, in NCDS.

Some analyses of parents' results against occupation, with the first five categories on the left of Figure 5.3 merged into one category (known as 'Outside the home'), and all the others merged into another category ('At home') were carried out. However, the numbers in the 'Outside the home' category were small (never more than 57), and partly for this reason, no doubt, none of the differences proved to be statistically significant; the results are therefore not reported.

Parents' qualifications

The parents' highest qualifications were classified in five categories ranging from 'below CSE/GCSE' to 'Higher education', and the distribution was as shown in Figure 5.4.

Figure 5.4: **Parents' highest qualification**

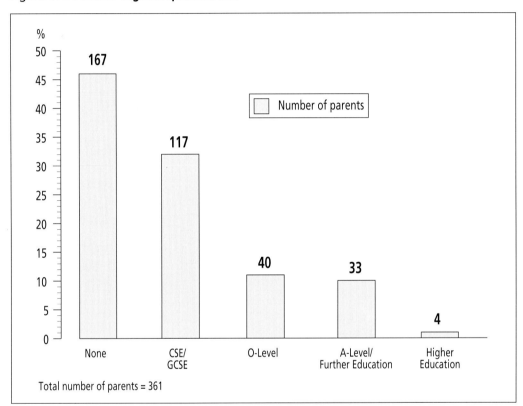

Total number of parents = 361

The great majority of those classified as having qualifications at CSE or GCSE level had one or two passes, at very low grades. Their level of qualification was barely above that of those reporting no qualifications at all. The further education qualifications were all practical certificates (in hairdressing, for example). One of the four graduates was a disabled person with a particular interest in acquiring computer skills, especially word-processing.

A comparison was made with the qualifications of the cohort members (men and women) in NCDS. They were all born in one week in 1958; many of them took O-Levels, CSEs or Scottish 'O' Grades in 1974, and some took A-Levels or Scottish Highers in 1976. In early 1992, when they were 33, they were asked whether they had any O-Levels or equivalent (including CSEs at Grade 1 and any O-Level passes at A-Level); of the 12,536 who answered the question, 7,636 or 61 per cent said they had, compared to 54 per cent in the Family Literacy sample who had at least one CSE or GCSE. The NCDS members were also asked if they had any A-Levels or equivalent; of the 7,654 who answered this question, 2,698 or 35 per cent said they had, compared to 11 per cent in the Family Literacy sample who had A-Level or further or higher education qualifications. In interpreting these comparisons, it must be borne in mind that:

- *the great majority of the Family Literacy parents were younger than 33*

- *during the 1970s and 1980s the proportion of 16- and 18-year-olds who took public examinations constantly increased*

- *the NCDS data for O-Level or equivalent include CSEs at Grade 1 but not below, while the Family Literacy figures for CSE/GCSE count any grade, even a 'G' in one subject.*

This would have increased the proportion of the Family Literacy sample who gained some qualification. The discrepancy in the qualifications of the two groups is therefore probably greater and more significant than it appears at first sight.

Analyses of Family Literacy parents' results were also carried out against level of qualifications, with 'below CSE/GCSE' treated as one category and all the rest merged. In this case the numbers in the two categories were much more evenly balanced, and several of the results were significant. These are reported in the sections on parents' reading and writing in this chapter and chapter 7.

At the start, the Programmes were joined by a few fairly well qualified parents. After one or two terms, the Programmes felt confident enough in their recruitment policies to begin to ask such people to stand down from a course in favour of those in more need. For instance, in one term one Programme recruited almost all the parents for a course at a non-central site through a one-off First Aid day at the end of the previous term. Even so, seven of the parents who had attended the First Aid course were considered ineligible for the Programme through being already well qualified. However, in another Programme, asking an able parent to stand down backfired on one occasion; she persuaded five others that the course was not for them either, and all six left.

The participating parents were therefore in general poorly qualified and not employed outside the home, and the Programmes were by design located in low-income, working-class areas. Since this was largely the target group the Agency had in mind, **the Programmes had in these respects been quite successful in their recruitment policy.**

5.2 The parents' aspirations

The aims and objectives set by the Agency were described in section 2.2, and the evaluation focused largely on the extent to which those aims and objectives were met. However, the success of an initiative should not be judged solely by the targets externally determined by funders and providers, however enlightened; it should be judged also in terms of what the participants hoped to get from it. In this case, information on what parents hoped they and their children would achieve was collected both through what parents wrote at the beginning of the course, and through what those interviewed during the course said.

5.2.1 The parents' aspirations for themselves

In writing

In what they wrote at the beginning of their course, the overwhelming majority of parents (90 per cent) said they wanted to **help their children to read and write.** To assist in this, many (44 per cent) wanted to acquire a greater understanding of **how children learn** and **what they learn** at school.

The second reason over half the parents (58 per cent) gave for enrolling was to **improve their own educational status** by improving their own **basic skills.** In many responses, helping children and improving their own skills were linked. Learning to use a computer was also often seen to be beneficial in both respects.

Some parents (10 per cent) enrolled (never primarily) with the idea of meeting others with similar interests; and some wanted to demonstrate by their involvement that they had the ability to complete a course with an educational emphasis. Several stressed the value of being able to spend uninterrupted time with their child. Others were glad of the opportunity offered to have a break from housework, while helping their child.

In interviews

In the interviews during the courses, parents were asked why they had decided to take part. The responses are summarised in Table 5.1.

Many parents gave **more than one reason**. In particular, the generic responses 'To help my children' and 'General personal improvement' rarely occurred alone. For example, responses classified as 'To help my children' cited either some perceived need(s) in the child, or some kind of semi-perceived need of the parent, usually accompanied by a commitment and an enthusiasm to do something about these perceptions. Also, responses classified as 'General personal improvement' cited a wide range of social or educational needs that the respondents had identified for themselves. Those most often cited are included in the table.

Table 5.1: **Why parents joined the course**

Cohort	Summer 1994	Autumn 1994	Spring 1995	Summer 1995	Total
Number of respondents	32	39	35	17	123
			Number of references		
To help my child(ren)	26	27	27	15	95
To gain patience/understanding	4	6	8	6	24
To get ideas	1	8	6	4	19
General encouragement for child	0	5	6	3	14
Specific learning difficulty with child	2	6	4	1	13
To improve child's reading	0	2	3	4	9
To improve child's writing	0	1	2	3	6
General personal improvement	13	9	10	8	40
To get a qualification	3	3	7	1	14
To gain confidence	1	8	3	1	13
To prepare for employment	4	5	3	0	12
For social sharing	1	5	3	1	10
Something to do	1	3	6	0	10
Parent's past educational difficulties	0	5	1	0	6

Some representative quotations from the parents were:

> *One reason was to help (my child). I wanted to understand how he would be taught at school so that I could help him at home. For myself, I wanted to learn how to use the word-processor so that again, I could help (child) when he started to use one. I also hoped that the course would prove to be a way of meeting other people and help to fill my time in.*

> *I thought it would benefit the children and at the same time, benefit me by learning more about how to help the children. I was especially interested in learning how to help [my children] with their reading and writing, as they had just started school.*

Thus the deciding factor mentioned by respondents from all Programmes and cohorts was to provide additional help for their children's development, including the felt need to keep up with their children's education. Some parents also mentioned their own learning. There were also other, scattered, references to the attraction of the activity base of the Programmes, including the word-processing aspect, and to the hope that the certification would help with job prospects. Some respondents were already helping at school and teachers had recommended the Programme to them as a way of improving what they could offer the children. For a few parents, crèche provision was the clinching reason – presumably as a prerequisite for being able to attend at all, rather than as an aspiration.

Only a very few parents hinted that their own problems with literacy were a prime reason for joining the Programme; for example, one said she was not very good at letter writing. That their own problems might be a sensitive issue for some parents was suggested by comments in one area when a local television presenter referred to the Programme as an 'adult **illiteracy** course' – the parents here (and elsewhere) were emphatic that these were adult **literacy** courses.

5.2.2 The parents' aspirations for their children

Relatively few parents directly stated their hopes for their children from the initiative, either in writing or during interview. There were some (rather general) references to hopes that their children would benefit, and a small number referred to particular problems that their children were experiencing at home. A worry that some parents might have had was hinted at by one parent in a follow-up interview:

> *We were worried about her before, before we went in we thought she's going to end up one of these delinquent children if I don't do something. She is so easily led though. We are trying to give her a bit more confidence obviously, so she doesn't do just as her friend says, so she can think for herself.*

However, the parents' hopes for their children were massively implied by the overwhelming preponderance, among their wishes for themselves, of the wish to be better equipped to help their children. It may be deduced that the aspiration that their children would benefit was the most powerful for almost all the parents.

A converging piece of evidence came from the information provided by the Programmes: **over 90 per cent of participating parents had never attended a basic skills course before**, despite such courses being available in all four areas. This was true even in the one Programme area where not only Adult Basic Skills courses but also nursery provision was widely available. Thus benefits simply for themselves had drawn only a very few of these parents into basic skills courses before. The inference to be drawn is that **the big attraction was helping their children.**

5.3 Parents' literacy levels

5.3.1 Writing: impression marks

Parents' writing was assessed holistically (impressionistically) on a seven-point scale. One example of writing from each of categories 2 to 7 is shown in Appendix A, subsection A.3.2. A score of 1 implied total or almost total inability to write, and is therefore not illustrated in the Appendix. Scores of 2 or 3 represented very low levels of attainment, at or possibly below Foundation level of the Agency's Communication Standards. Scores of 4 and above show a basic but still low competence in communicating in writing, predominantly at level 1 of the Standards (a few of those with scores of 7 would be at level 2). Across the range of scores from 4 to 7, the differences between scripts were in terms of greater length, increasing control over content and handwriting, and fewer errors in grammar, spelling and style.

The distribution of parents' general impression scores at the beginning of the course, on this seven-point scale and summing across the four cohorts, was as shown in Figure 5.5, where the average score and standard deviation (s.d.) are also shown. The standard deviation is a measure of the spread of scores associated with each mean

Figure 5.5: **Distribution of general impression scores, and average score, for parents' writing: beginning of course**

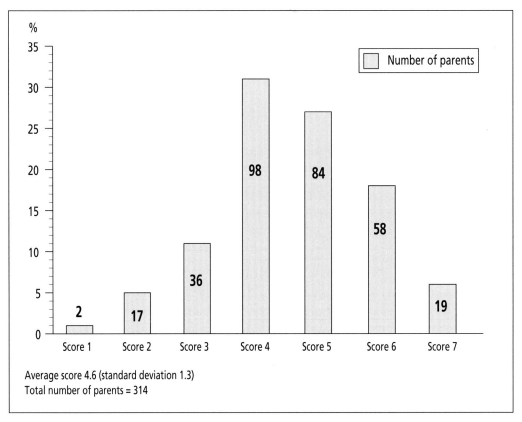

Average score 4.6 (standard deviation 1.3)
Total number of parents = 314

score. This measure is discussed in more detail in the context of the Peabody test results later in this chapter and in chapter 6.

There were therefore **very few people in this sample who were unable to write at all.** There were also relatively few with the very low levels of attainment represented by scores of 2 or 3. The great majority had basic but low competence in writing, but their scripts typically showed poor to moderate control over grammar, spelling and style. Such levels would help to explain both the low level of confidence on parents' part in their abilities, and the strength of their desire to improve them.

The analysis according to parents' level of qualifications showed that those with any formal qualification at all had a significantly higher mean score (4.8; s.d. = 1.2; N = 172) than those with no qualifications (mean score = 4.3; s.d. = 1.3; N = 142).

5.3.2 Reading

As a measure of their reading ability, parents were asked to complete a three-part cloze (gap-filling) test. The test is reproduced in Appendix D. The average scores on the three parts of the test at the beginning of the course, summing across the four cohorts, were as shown in Table 5.2.

Table 5.2: **Parents' cloze test (reading) scores: beginning of course**

	N	mean score		
		raw	(s.d.)	%
Part 1 (maximum = 11)	209	8.8	(1.8)	80
Part 2 (maximum = 17)	257	12.6	(2.5)	74
Part 3 (maximum = 34)	353	22.6	(4.8)	66

Key: N = sample size;   s.d. = standard deviation

Throughout the evaluation, fewer parents took part 1 of the test than part 2, and fewer took part 2 than part 3. This appeared to reflect decisions by Programme staff not to put some parents through a test that would not challenge them, and/or to make best use of limited testing time (especially at follow-ups). The set of tests as a whole was found to have been pitched at an appropriate range of difficulty; success rates at the beginning of the courses ranged from 66 to 80 per cent. In order to allow this rate of success, the individual items in the tests were mainly simple.

The numbers and percentages of parents who achieved less than half-marks on each of the cloze tests at the beginning of the courses were as follows:

Test	Number of parents	%
1	12	6
2	21	8
3	27	8

Thus the numbers of parents who achieved very low initial scores on these tests, even Part 3, were small. This was consistent both with the high average scores on these tests, and with the small numbers who had very low initial scores in writing. Given the simple overall level of the tests, however, the general level of the parents' reading ability was modest.

The analysis according to parents' level of qualifications showed that those with qualifications had significantly higher mean scores on all three parts of the test than those with no qualifications . The details were as follows:

Test	Parents without qualifications			Parents with qualifications		
	N	mean score	(s.d.)	N	mean score	(s.d.)
1	107	8.3	(2.0)	102	9.3	(1.4)
2	140	12.2	(2.8)	117	13.1	(2.0)
3	172	21.5	(5.3)	181	23.7	(3.9)

Key: N = sample size; s.d. = standard deviation

5.3.3 Communication Standards levels

The Programmes also provided information on the numbers of parents whom they judged to be at various levels of the Agency's Communication Standards at the beginning of the courses. This information is summarised in Figure 5.6.

Figure 5.6: **Parents' Communication Standards levels: beginning of course**

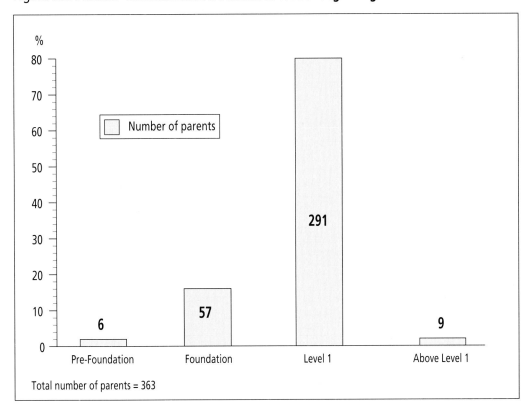

Total number of parents = 363

This distribution was again consistent with the picture given by the initial scores for reading and writing. **Most parents came to the courses with low communication abilities in written English** (level 1), about a sixth with very low skills (Foundation level), and very few with either basic abilities (above level 1) or almost none (pre-Foundation). All of those at level 1 or below would be thought of as having low literacy skills, and therefore within that sixth of the population mentioned at the beginning of this report, and validly targeted by the Programmes.

However, only 18 per cent were at or below Foundation level, and this contrasts with the objective set by the Agency (see section 2.2) that at least 30 per cent of participating parents should be at or below Foundation level on entry. As a coordinator commented in an interview, 'In general it's the ones that are not coming who need more help and that's a hard one to get across.'

But it may be that that objective was unrealistic. The apparently widespread view that a substantial proportion of the population have almost no literacy (as opposed to *low* literacy) is not borne out by research. For instance, the *On the Move* adult literacy initiative, mounted by the Agency's predecessor body and the BBC in the mid-1970s, was planned on the assumption that large numbers of virtually illiterate people would come forward. However, the evaluation (Gorman and Moss, 1979; Gorman, 1981) showed that only about 10 per cent of those who came forward could be so classified. The great majority were people who had basic but low literacy, knew that that was insufficient, and were strongly motivated to improve. Similarly, from research projects both in the early 1970s (see Rogers, 1986) and the 1990s (see Ekinsmyth and Bynner, 1994, p.20, Figure 2.2) it could be estimated that only about one per cent of the adult population were illiterate. So it may be that, even in areas of multiple deprivation, within 'catchment' distance of any one Family Literacy site the majority would be at level 1, but there would be an important minority at Foundation level.

There was a little evidence that rather more Foundation level parents began to volunteer in some places as the Programmes became better known. This was the view of most of the coordinators – but they also emphasised that this was happening mainly at Programmes' main sites. One Adult Basic Skills Coordinator said:

> *I think probably the reason that we are getting the Foundation levels is that ... they are in our base school, parents are getting to hear about us more from other parents and they know that they can come on this course and not feel thick, they will enjoy it and get a lot out of it. But I think that as regards the new school where we had such a lot (of Foundation level students) coming in straight away I think it must be because of the school's attitude to parents and the staff are very encouraging there, before we even went in and tried to get the parents to come along. And I think there's also the little groups of friends – if one came the others came as well, which helped.*

So where Foundation-level parents were recruited the reasons seemed to be that such parents needed to know either that a course had been going for some time and that their friends had been on it and benefited, or that their children's school was recommending it, and above all that they themselves would be welcomed onto it and not made to feel deficient. For them the barrier to enrolling was very difficult to cross. If this analysis is correct, it has implications for the use of changing or continuing sites (see section 11.4).

The evidence on parents' literacy levels at the beginning of the courses shows that **the great majority of parents entered with low attainment, and themselves needing to improve.**

5.4 Literacy-related home activities

Information on literacy-related activities in the home was gathered through the Home Activities questionnaire, and the full data are given in Appendix B. Inspection of the figures for the beginning of the course revealed the following picture of literacy-related home activities before participation. The great majority of parents were **already looking at books**, and not only watching TV but also talking about it, **with their children every day**; and every day the great majority of children would **tell their parents what they had done at school**, and **write their name** for them. Joint activities that occurred at least once a week on average were:

- *looking at magazines*
- *shopping*
- *drawing or painting*
- *cutting and sticking*
- *the making up of stories (by both parents and children)*
- *using a real or toy telephone*
- *singing songs or nursery rhymes, and*
- *the parent reading a story to the child.*

Activities that were rare on average included: looking at newspapers and TV guides, letters, photo albums and religious material together, using a computer, making a scrapbook, and borrowing children's books from a library. The great majority of parents claimed that their children had over 20 books of their own. **Thus there were familiar activities to form the basis for the extension of others.** Similar findings were reported by Weinberger (1995); she also found, however, that the 'home curriculum' needed to come into relationship with the school approach, and that this in turn required that teachers acknowledge the home curriculum.

It was possible to compare the responses of parents in the Programmes with those of mothers in the NCDS sample in relation to two questions. These concerned the number of books a child owned and the frequency with which parents read to their child. An analysis of NCDS data has shown that both of those variables have a highly significant relationship to children's scores on the PPVT (Gorman and Hutchison, forthcoming).

Eighty-one per cent of the NCDS sample and 76 per cent of the Family Literacy group claimed to read stories to their children three times a week or more. In this respect the two sets of responses were similar. This was also the case for the number of books owned by the children. Seventy-eight per cent of the NCDS sample and 73 per cent of the Family Literacy parents reported that their child was the owner of over 20 books. More specifically, 35 per cent of the NCDS sample and over 40 per cent of the Family

Literacy parents said that their child owned over 50 books. As this evidence was obtained near the start of the Family Literacy courses, it indicates that the parents involved had an interest in their child's literacy development that was at least as great as those of parents generally.

Other evidence obtained from the Programmes suggests that the majority of the Family Literacy parents already had contacts with their children's schools and teachers which were more frequent and educationally focused than was generally the case. For example, virtually all the Family Literacy parents (94 per cent) said they had talked to their child's teacher, 85 per cent had been involved in school activities, and over half had helped out in such activities. In contrast, nearly half of the parents in the NCDS sample had **not** attended any school events in the year of the survey, over two-thirds had **not** discussed their child with a teacher that year, and a similar proportion had **not** 'joined the school day' for any purpose.

The high level of involvement of parents in the Programmes with their children's schools will also be a reflection of the desire of heads and teachers to encourage parental involvement in their life of the schools. The majority of the schools hosting literacy projects were notable in this respect. On their part, most of the parents in the programmes responded positively and enthusiastically to the opportunities provided for contacts with their children's teachers and for involvement in school activities.

5.5 Children's language and literacy levels

5.5.1 Writing

A scale for the categorisation of children's writing was developed on the basis of extensive experience in the field and of the characteristics of the samples of children's writing or emergent writing gathered.

The samples were classified into seven stages:

1. Story-related drawings, and sign-writing

2. Letter-like forms

3. Copying letters

4. Child's name and strings of letters

5. Words

6. One or more clauses or sentences

7. A written text including a coherent series of clauses or sentences, and showing control of letter formation (size and shape), of word division, and of left to right orientation.

Examples of each stage, with commentary and guidance for parents and teachers, can be found in Gorman and Brooks (1996).

The distribution of children on the stages of this scale, at the beginning of the courses and summing across the four cohorts, was as shown in Figure 5.7. Also shown in the Figure is the average calculated by treating the stages as points on an equal-interval ordinal scale.

The very small number of children at stage 3 means that this is a stage that most children pass through very quickly.

Within the developmental scale, the most crucial transition is that from stage 4 to stage 5. This is because up to stage 4 children are attaching very little meaning to the individual marks on the paper, whereas from stage 5 onwards they are communicating linguistic meaning in writing. That is, from stage 5 onwards they are literate, at first only in the most basic sense but ever more fully thereafter.

Figure 5.7: **Distribution of children's writing across developmental stages: beginning of course**

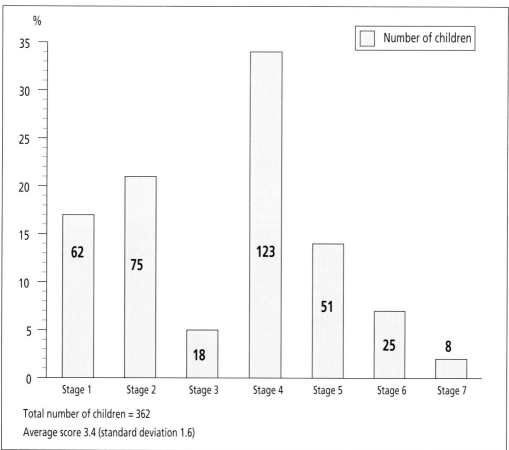

Figure 5.7 shows that at the beginning of the courses **only 23 per cent of these children had made the vital transition to communicating meaning in writing**. However, that Table takes no account of the children's ages; an analysis of the distribution of writing stages according to children's ages was therefore carried out. Children who were over 5 at the beginning of the course were of an age to have started school. While it would not be expected that every child in these groups would have begun to write words, the proportion of these children who **had** made the transition to stage 5 (38 per cent) was very low. Even among six-year-olds **a substantial proportion (34 per cent) were still below the minimum writing level necessary for making progress in the curriculum.**

5.5.2 Vocabulary and reading

For each child aged 4:00-6:11 at the beginning of the course the PPVT data provided a raw score. These raw scores were then converted into standardised scores by using the results from the 2385 children tested on the PPVT in NCDS as the standardisation set.

Similarly, for each child aged 5:00-6:11 at the beginning of the course the PIAT data provided raw scores, and these were processed in the same way as the PPVT scores, against the scores of the 2617 children tested on the PIAT in NCDS.

The mean standardised scores (and s.d's) for the two tests, for the beginning of the courses and summing across the four cohorts, were as shown in Table 5.3. The Table also gives the national averages, and the mean scores for the nearest comparable group of children in NCDS (for how these scores were calculated, see Appendix A, section A.4.2). The distributions of scores are illustrated in Figures 5.8 and 5.9 for the PPVT and the PIAT respectively; in both cases the 'normal' curve is shown for comparison.

Table 5.3: **Children's vocabulary and reading scores (Peabody tests): beginning of course**

	N	Mean stand-ardised score	(s.d.)	National average	Average of nearest NCDS group
Vocabulary (PPVT)	330	84.8	(13.0)	100.0	95.7
Reading (PIAT)	180	83.6	(16.2)	100.0	93.2

Key: N = sample size; s.d. = standard deviation

Figure 5.8: Distribution curves for PPVT scores of Family Literacy sample, beginning of course and nationally

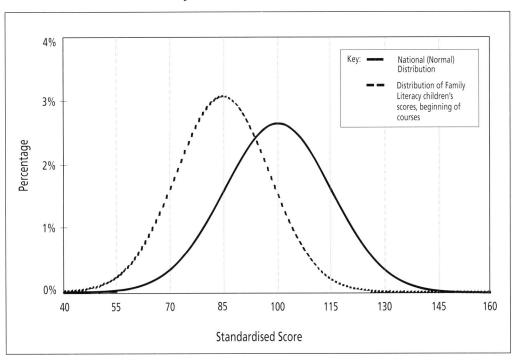

In a normal Gaussian or 'bell curve' distribution, such as that for the NCDS standardisation set used here, the mean is set by definition at 100, and the standard deviation at 15. Just over two-thirds (68 per cent) of all scores fall between plus or minus one standard deviation, with just under one-sixth (16 per cent) above plus one s.d. (115) and the remaining 16 per cent below minus one s.d. (85). Furthermore, 95 per cent of all scores fall between plus or minus two standard deviations, with 2.5 per cent above plus two s.d.'s (130) and the remaining 2.5 per cent below minus two s.d.'s (70).

In less technical language, children who score between 85 and 115 are often described as in the 'average range'. Those who score above 115 are able, and those below 85 are struggling. In a normal distribution, 16 per cent fall into each of these categories. Those who score above 130 are highly able, and those below 70 are severely disadvantaged for learning. In a normal distribution, only one child in 40 falls into each of these groups.

For the sample of children in this evaluation, on both tests **the averages for the beginning of term were substantially below the national average**; in fact, rather more than a complete s.d. below. The averages were also considerably below those of the most closely comparable group of children in NCDS. In the graphs, the difference between this sample and a normally-distributed one shows as a substantial shift to the left in the curve for the Family Literacy children. What this means in non-technical terms is disturbing. In a normal distribution, just under one-sixth (17 per cent) are below 85, and struggling; in this sample, **the proportion below 85, and struggling, was over half** (54 per cent on the PPVT, 67 per cent on the PIAT). Only seven and 10 children (two and six per cent) respectively were above 115.

Figure 5.9: **Distribution curves for PIAT scores of Family Literacy sample, beginning of course and nationally**

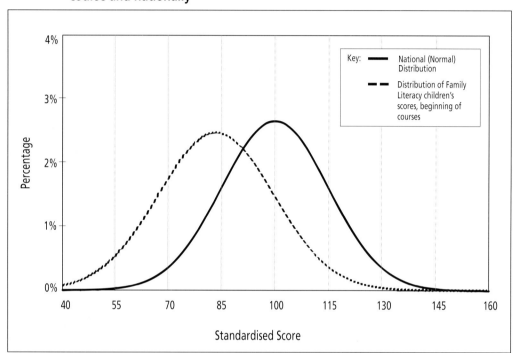

And inspection of the full distribution of scores showed that the position of some of these children at the beginning of the courses was even worse than just implied. In a normal distribution, 2.5 per cent (one in 40) are below 70, and severely disadvantaged for learning; in this sample, **the proportion below 70, and severely disadvantaged for learning, was 17 per cent, or one child in every six, on the PPVT, and 24 per cent, or one child in every four, on the PIAT.** At the other extreme, above 130, there were just two children (less than one per cent), on the PPVT, and three (two per cent) on the PIAT.

These tests are measures of vocabulary and reading development. These abilities are vital for education and for life, and the heavily depressed scores of so many of these children meant that **they had not yet acquired much of the foundation of vocabulary and early reading skills necessary for progress in other areas.**

And the story did not end there. In all standardisation exercises, there are too few children outside the range 70-130 to base further calculation of standardised scores on; so these children are said simply to be 'above 130' or 'below 70'. When calculating the average score of a tested group, such children are given scores of 131 and 69 respectively. And in a sample with a distribution that is anywhere near normal, there are so few such children that giving them these 'inaccurate' standardised scores hardly affects the calculation of the average; in any case the extremes largely cancel each other out.

But in this sample, on the PPVT there were just two children who were given the 'shadow' score of 131, while there were 57 who were given 69. On the PIAT the numbers were three and 43. The implication is that **even the already low averages of 84.8 and 83.6 were probably too high**, because many of the children who were attributed standardised scores of 69 should in theory have had much lower scores.

It would be true, but a gross understatement, to say that these children were validly targeted. They were validly targeted, since, as a group, their vocabulary, reading and writing attainments were seriously below average before they and their parents participated in the Programme. But it would much closer to the justified emphasis to say that **the great majority of these children were in very urgent need of help to reduce their high risk of educational failure**.

If these parents were already so strongly motivated on their children's behalf, and already so involved in literacy-related activities with them, then why, it might be asked, were their children performing so poorly? A strong possibility, based on her own detailed research on similar families, was suggested by Snow (1994, p.267): such parents may not know how 'to ensure that the full benefits of book reading are made accessible to young children, especially those most at risk of school failure'. This barrier would need to be overcome if the children, and the parents themselves, were to benefit fully from the Programmes.

5.6 Summary

- The parents who were recruited onto these Programmes were validly targeted: they were **poorly qualified**, lived in areas of **multiple deprivation**, and had **low levels of literacy**.

- Fewer parents whose skills were below level 1 of the Agency's Communication Standards were recruited than the Agency had specified; but this may have been because there were fewer such parents in the courses' catchment areas than had been thought. Some success was achieved in recruiting greater numbers of such parents over time, particularly at continuing sites.

- Despite (or perhaps in part because of) their own literacy problems, the parents brought to the Programmes a vital prerequisite for their own and their children's success: **strong motivation on their children's behalf**. This was shown by the hopes they expressed or implied, by the literacy-related activities they were already engaged in at home, and by their involvement with their children's schools.

- **Most of their children were disadvantaged for learning by low scores in language and literacy, at great risk of educational failure, and in urgent need of help.**

The next three chapters document the progress made by parents and children from these low starting points.

CHAPTER SIX

Children's progress in language and literacy

6.1 Vocabulary development

In this chapter and in chapter 8, the performance results for children and parents respectively are presented on the basis of 'returners', that is, those who returned for testing on the various relevant occasions. (For total numbers of those who took the tests on each occasion, regardless of whether they returned on subsequent occasions, and for discussion of using returners rather than all test-takers, see Appendix A, section A.9.) The PPVT results for the children who returned for testing, and summing across cohorts, were as shown in Table 6.1. The national average and the nearest NCDS average are shown for comparison. The distributions of scores at three of the four occasions of testing are illustrated in Figure 6.1; the 'normal' curve is shown for comparison.

Table 6.1: **Children's listening vocabulary (PPVT) scores: returners only**

N	Beginning of course		End of course		12-week follow-up		9-month follow-up	
	mean	(s.d.)	mean	(s.d.)	mean	(s.d.)	mean	(s.d.)
330	84.8	(13.0)						
273	**85.0**	(13.1)	**89.8**	(13.7)				
192	86.0	(13.5)	**91.3**	(14.2)	**93.0**	(14.9)		
112	85.4	(12.6)	90.7	(13.5)	**92.9**	(14.5)	**93.0**	(15.3)

N.B.   National average = 100.0; average score of nearest comparable group in NCDS = 95.7

Key: N = sample size;   s.d. = standard deviation

In Table 6.1 (and similarly in all subsequent performance data Tables):

- *the most important comparison in each line is between the two scores in **bold***

- *the first line gives the number, mean score and s.d. of all those tested at the **beginning** of the course (from all four cohorts)*

> • *the second line gives the number of all those tested at **both the end and the beginning** of a course (from all four cohorts), with their means and s.d's for both occasions*

> • *the third line gives the number of all those tested at **12-week follow-up and both previous occasions** (from the first three cohorts), with their means and s.d's for all three occasions*

> • *the fourth line gives the number of all those tested at **9-month follow-up and all three previous occasions** (from the first two cohorts), with their means and s.d's for all four occasions.*

Figure 6.1: **Distribution curves for PPVT scores of Family Literacy sample for three occasions of testing, and nationally**

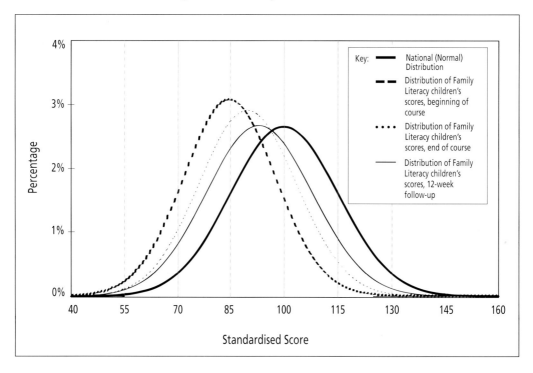

In the second column of Table 6.1 there is some evidence of differential attrition. That is, the scores for the beginning of the course showed a tendency to rise as fewer children returned for testing on later occasions and only their scores were used to re-calculate the beginning-of-course scores; the tendency for previous averages to rise when re-calculated means that some of the children who did not return for re-testing were among those with the lowest original scores. This tendency is clearest in the third line of the table; for the children who returned for testing at the 12-week follow-up, the re-calculated average for the beginning of the course was distinctly higher than the average calculated originally. The fourth line shows that the 9-month follow-up children's average for the beginning of term was still higher than the original figure, even though it had tended back towards that figure. Some differential attrition had therefore occurred; the implications of this are discussed in section 6.3 below.

For the reasons already implied (different numbers of cohorts; differential attrition), comparisons between mean scores in the same *column* of Table 6.1 are unjustified. Comparisons need to be made between mean scores in the same *row*. In order to interpret those comparisons, statistical tests of the differences were carried out. Though the major comparison of interest in each row is between the two scores picked out in bold, statistical tests of all the differences between pairs of means in each row were carried out.

For the results presented in Table 6.1, **all** differences between means in the same row were statistically significant (p<0.05), except the difference between the two follow-ups in line 4. Thus the end of course mean was higher than the beginning of course mean in all three calculations (lines 2-4 of the Table). **This shows that these children made substantial progress in vocabulary during the course relative to NCDS, and therefore greater progress than would have been expected solely from normal development.**

The differences between the end of term and 12-week follow-up means were significant in both relevant calculations. **Therefore the children concerned continued to make greater than expected progress in vocabulary in the 12 weeks after the course.**

Both of these significant improvements show up clearly in Figure 6.1, in the steady shifting to the right of the curves for this sample over time.

There was no difference between the two follow-up means (in line 4 of the Table). This does **not** mean that these children had stopped progressing, only that in the 6 months between the two follow-ups they had made only the expected amount of progress, and at the 9-month follow-up were still at the same relative level as 6 months earlier. **They had sustained the greater than expected progress in vocabulary already made during the course and in the 12 weeks after it, and continued to make 'normal' progress.** Since the 9-month follow-up mean had not fallen, there was no evidence of 'wash-out', that is, of the previous gains being lost. Indeed, for such a disadvantaged group of children to make 'normal' progress could be seen as positive. Only a further follow-up study could determine whether they continued to hold their own in the longer term.

The comparison with NCDS shows that, even at the 9-month follow-up, these children still had an average score somewhat below that of the most closely comparable group, that is, they still on average lagged behind their peers in the wider community.

Three evaluations in the United States which also used the PPVT provided other comparisons. In a pilot family literacy project in Hawai'i, in which participants enrolled for a year, 'children improved their average percentile performance from 36 to 43' on the national norms for the United States (Hayes, undated, p.28), but no test of the significance of this result was reported. The National Center for Family Literacy (undated, p.17) found that, over the course of a year, the average position of children in the Toyota Families for Learning programme moved up from the 11th to the 19th percentile, and that the improvement was significant. Similarly, in the national evaluation of Even Start, after participating for (on average) seven months, children were found a further nine months later to have moved up on average from the ninth to the 19th percentile, and their average standardised score had risen from 76.6 to 83.7, also a significant improvement (St. Pierre *et al.*, 1995, pp.169-71). All three studies showed the same trend for children to make greater-than-expected gains as in the Family Literacy Programmes.

6.2 Early reading attainment

The results for the PIAT, calculated on the 'returners' basis and summing across cohorts, were as shown in Table 6.2. The national average and the nearest NCDS average are shown for comparison. The distributions of scores at three of the four occasions of testing are illustrated in Figure 6.2; the 'normal' curve is shown for comparison.

The second column of Table 6.2 on the next page again shows some evidence of differential attrition, though less marked than in the case of the PPVT results.

All the differences between pairs of mean scores in the same row were statistically significant ($p < 0.05$), except:

> - *in line 3, that between the end of term and the 12-week follow-up*

> - *in line 4, those between the 9-month follow-up on the one hand and both the end of term and the 12-week follow-up on the other.*

Thus the end of course mean was higher than the beginning of course mean in all three calculations (lines 2-4 of the Table). **This shows that these children also made substantial progress in reading during the course relative to NCDS, and therefore again greater progress than would have been expected solely from normal development.**

Table 6.2: **Children's reading (PIAT) scores: returners only**

N	Beginning of course		End of course		12-week follow-up		9-month follow-up	
	mean	(s.d.)	mean	(s.d.)	mean	(s.d.)	mean	(s.d.)
180	83.6	(16.2)						
147	**84.1**	(17.0)	**88.5**	(17.9)				
101	85.6	(17.6)	**90.6**	(17.2)	**92.4**	(17.5)		
67	84.2	(16.2)	88.7	(15.2)	**91.8**	(16.3)	**90.3**	(18.1)

N.B.   National average = 100.0; average score of nearest comparable group in NCDS = 93.2

Key: N = sample size;   s.d. = standard deviation

The difference between the end of term and 12-week follow-up means was significant in line 4 of the Table (that is, for the Summer and Autumn 1994 cohorts), but not in line 3 (that is, for those two cohorts plus the Spring 1995 cohort). **The gain in reading made during the course was therefore being sustained, and for some children was being improved on further.**

Again, the significant improvements show up in Figure 6.2, over the page, in the steady shifting of the curves to the right.

Despite the apparent fall, the difference between the two follow-up means was not significant. **The gains in reading made during the course (and by some children immediately after it) were being sustained,** and there was no definite evidence of wash-out. The absence of a further rise in the standardised mean score does not mean that these children had made no progress in the six months between the two follow-ups; they had, in 'absolute' terms, but were still at about the same *relative* level as they had been six months earlier. And again, a further follow-up study would be needed to determine whether the gains continued to be sustained in the longer term.

Again, even at the 9-month follow-up, these children had an average score somewhat below that of the most closely comparable group in NCDS, and were therefore still on average behind their peers in the wider community.

Figure 6.2: **Distribution curves for PIAT scores of Family Literacy sample for three occasions of testing, and nationally**

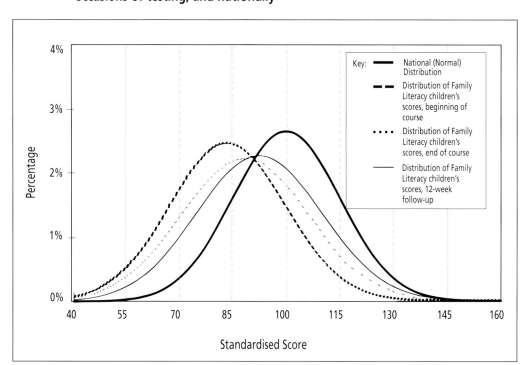

6.3 Non-technical comment on the Peabody test results

In chapter 5, an attempt was made to comment on the Peabody results for the beginning of the courses in non-technical terms, and a corresponding attempt will be made here to discuss the further results similarly.

The most important feature of the results in Tables 6.1 and 6.2 is that the gap between the average scores and the standardised mean of 100 had narrowed considerably over time (that is, from left to right along each line of both Tables), especially during the courses. What this meant in terms of the proportions in the 'average range' and on either side can be summarised as follows:

On the PPVT:

- *at the beginning of the courses, the proportion below 70 ('severely disadvantaged for learning') was 17 per cent; by the end of the courses, this had fallen to 10 per cent, and by the 12-week follow-up, to six per cent*

- *at the beginning of the courses, the proportion below 85 ('struggling') was 54 per cent; by the end of the courses, this had fallen to 40 per cent, and by the 12-week follow-up, to 31 per cent*

- *at the beginning of the courses, the proportion between 85 and 115 ('average range') was 44 per cent; by the end of the courses, this had risen to 59 per cent, and by the 12-week follow-up, to 63 per cent*

- *at the beginning of the courses, the proportion above 115 ('able') was two per cent; by the end of the courses, this had risen to five per cent, and by the 12-week follow-up, to eight per cent.*

On the PIAT:

- *at the beginning of the courses, the proportion below 70 was 24 per cent; by the end of the courses, this had fallen to 19 per cent, and by the 12-week follow-up, to nine per cent*

- *at the beginning of the courses, the proportion below 85 was 67 per cent; by the end of the courses, this had fallen to 52 per cent, and by the 12-week follow-up, to 35 per cent*

- *at the beginning of the courses, the proportion between 85 and 115 was 29 per cent; by the end of the courses, this had risen to 41 per cent, and by the 12-week follow-up, to 55 per cent*

- *at the beginning of the courses, the proportion above 115 was six per cent; by the end of the courses, this had risen to eight per cent, and by the 12-week follow-up, to 12 per cent.*

Another important feature of the PPVT results (Table 6.1) is the tendency for the standard deviations to increase over time (again, this means from left to right along each **line** of the Table). This tendency is less marked in the PIAT results (Table 6.2), but is clear for the 9-month follow-up in line 4. This trend means that for both tests the spread of scores tended to increase; and that in turn means that, while some children made good progress, others made less progress and therefore were being left, relatively, ever further behind.

The differential attrition in the samples returning for testing has already been pointed out. This is not just a statistical matter; it appears to mean that some of the children who did not return for testing were among those who had the lowest original scores, and were therefore in greatest need. For children who did not return, later scores are by definition not known; therefore it is logically possible that these children could have made good progress. But it seems more likely that they would have made less progress than the generality of those who did return for testing.

The rising mean scores suggested that **the initiative was working for the great majority of children.** However, the increasing spread of scores, and the differential attrition, suggested that **for some children in greatest need it was working less well** – and it may be that only highly intensive, individual remedial programmes would work for them.

Four conclusions follow:

> • *after the courses, most of the children who had made gains had sustained them; and since most of the children who took tests were in school by the time of the 9-month follow-up if not earlier, it would appear that their schools, as well as their families, were enabling them to maintain their gains*

> • *a few children were benefiting significantly less than the majority, and might be in need of even more help*

> • *many children were still well below average on both vocabulary and reading, but*

> • ***many more children than at the beginning of the courses would have at least adequate vocabulary and reading for learning in school.***

6.4 Early writing development

The average scores for children's writing on the seven-point developmental scale, for those who returned for testing on each occasion and summing across cohorts, were as shown in Table 6.3 on the next page.

The rises in average scores in the second column again show that those children who had lower scores at the beginning increasingly did not return at re-tests. However, in contrast to the Peabody results, there was no tendency here for the standard deviation to increase over time – therefore there seemed to be no evidence of children with lower initial scores being left relatively further behind in writing.

All the differences between pairs of mean scores in the same row were statistically significant ($p < 0.05$), including the three pairs of means of crucial importance (those in bold). Therefore **these children made substantial progress in writing both during the** courses, and in the 12 weeks following them, and in the six months between the two follow-ups.

Table 6.3: **Average scores for children's writing: returners only**

N	Beginning of course		End of course		12-week follow-up		9-month follow-up	
	mean	(s.d.)	mean	(s.d.)	mean	(s.d.)	mean	(s.d.)
362	3.4	(1.6)						
279	**3.5**	(1.6)	**4.1**	(1.7)				
179	3.7	(1.6)	**4.3**	(1.6)	**4.6**	(1.4)		
91	4.0	(1.5)	4.4	(1.5)	**4.8**	(1.3)	**5.4**	(1.3)

Key: N = sample size;   s.d. = standard deviation

Part of each of these improvements would have occurred in any case; any rise in non-standardised scores such as these must be partly due to children's general development and schooling. However, since it occurred alongside better-than-expected improvements in the standardised vocabulary and reading scores, and many of the children were not in school at the time, **most of the improvement during the courses can be attributed to the Programmes.** Since no standardised or even nationally representative data for the progress in writing of children of this age-range exist, it is impossible to quantify the separate contributions of the Programmes on the one hand, and of maturation and schooling on the other. However, **it was the researchers' judgement that these children made much more progress in writing during the courses than they would have made otherwise.**

Moreover, the progress made during the courses was built upon after them, and the **further improvements in writing at the follow-ups also seemed to represent distinctly more progress than would have been expected** simply from growth and schooling.

It was stated in chapter 5 that, on the seven-point developmental scale for children's writing used in this study, the crucial transition is that from stage 4 to stage 5. Analyses according to children's ages were therefore carried out, and Table 6.4 presents the proportions of children at stages 5 and above for the four occasions of testing, by age-bands from age 4:00 upwards. (Very few children aged below 4:00 were asked to provide samples of emergent writing, and it would not be expected that many of them would move beyond stage 4 during the timescale of the evaluation.)

Table 6.4: **Percentages of children at writing stage 5 and above at four occasions of testing, by age at beginning of course**

Age at beginning of course	Percentage of children at stage 5 or above			
	Beginning of course	End of course	12-week follow-up	9-month follow-up
4:00-4:05	2	21	28	(n/a)
4:06-4:11	17	42	54	39
5:00-5:05	19	47	50	50
5:06-5:11	28	51	51	83
6:00-6:05	60	71	67	79
6:06-6:11	76	67	76	85

Key:　(n/a)　too few children tested to make percentage reliable

Thus there was a generally rising trend in the proportion of children who had reached or passed stage 5. Differential attrition was almost certainly the explanation of the few exceptions to that trend. During the courses, the proportion of children aged 5:00 and over at the beginning who had not yet made the transition to stage 5 fell from 62 per cent to 43 per cent.

As already signalled in the discussion of Table 6.3, part of these improvements would have occurred in any case. Also, some children were not making much progress. Nevertheless, the overall trend was clear, and positive; **the proportions of children adequately equipped in writing for the demands of the school curriculum were steadily rising.** Moreover, the schools and the children's families appeared to be building on the improvement in writing achieved by the children during the courses.

Differences in vocabulary development, reading attainment and writing attainment between boys and girls were investigated. No significant differences were found at any stage of testing; boys and girls started about equal in all three aspects of language and literacy, and remained so.

Overall, therefore, in **vocabulary, reading and writing the children had received a boost to their achievement**, either just before or very early in their school career. If the longitudinal effects for them are similar to those found for the people born in 1970 and studied by Bynner and Steedman (1995), then this should benefit them in the very long term.

6.5　Parents' views on their children's progress

All parents who completed the writing tasks at the end of the course and at the two follow-ups were asked to write about any changes they had seen in their children, and many mentioned their children's progress. And those who were interviewed during the course and at follow-ups were asked explicitly whether they had noticed any changes in their children's talking, reading and writing.

In what parents **wrote at the end of the course** the largest set of responses (41 per cent) referred to a perceptible change in the child's **attitudes to learning**. One parent simply remarked: 'She concentrates more.' Others were more specific. Many parents (28 per cent) wrote about their child's gain **in confidence** in different respects, such as confidence in collaborating with others in a group, confidence in carrying out tasks given to them and confidence in communicating with others. Many parents said that their child had enjoyed the experience of learning alongside them. One aspect that was commented on by about one in ten parents (11 per cent) was the **desire of children to continue at home the relationship they had formed with their parent as mentor or guide.**

Over one in four parents referred to **improvements in their child's reading** (29 per cent) **or writing** (27 per cent) and about one in five (18 per cent) mentioned an **improvement in their child's speaking** or communicating. Several used the term 'more outspoken' in this connection. One simply remarked: 'He asks more questions.' A similar proportion (18 per cent) referred to an increase in the extent to which their child was involved in **creative activities** of different kinds.

A further eight per cent said that their child had learnt letters or numbers. Others (four per cent) referred to an improvement in their child's hand-control or coordination at the end of the course. Such remarks would tend to be made by the parents of children who were at a relatively early stage of literacy development.

In the **12-week follow-up study**, the proportions of parents commenting positively in relation to the main categories of response were generally similar to those given at the end of the course. However, there were two aspects on which even larger proportions of parents responded positively after 12 weeks than at the earlier stage. These related to the **continued growth** in their child's **self-confidence** and **reading ability**. A third of the parents responding (34 per cent) said that their child's reading had continued to improve and four out of ten parents (42 per cent) commented on their continued growth in confidence. (At the end of the course, the proportions were 29 per cent and 28 per cent respectively.)

In the **9-month follow-up**, the proportions of positive responses were very similar to those given at the 12-week follow-up. In two respects, the proportion noting continued improvement was smaller than at the end of course (in the child's speaking or listening, nine per cent as opposed to 18 per cent; in their child's writing and spelling, 19 per cent as opposed to 27 per cent). From the perspective of the parents, therefore, positive gains made by the child as a consequence of the course largely continued to be apparent nine months after the course.

Across the 123 **interviews** with parents during the courses over the four terms, there were 134 references to an **improvement in children's talking** (that is, some parents mentioned this more than once). Even though many of these references were to the parent's improved communication with the child, and therefore as much to the parent's own improvement in communication and in ability to notice the child's ability, this indicates a great deal of improvement that had come to parents' attention. Within the 123 interviews there were also 43 references to improvements in children's reading, and 60 to improvements in children's writing.

When asked directly about benefits to their children, the parents who were interviewed found the questions somewhat difficult, perhaps mainly because they had just been asked whether the courses had helped them to help their children better, and the answers tended to overlap. However, with reference to her children's **talking** one parent spoke for many when she said: 'Yes. We can't shut them up now.' Some parents claimed not to have identified any gain, some having children who were already 'good at talking'. At the opposite extreme, one parent reported: '(My child) was a late talker... Since ... joining the course his speech has improved a lot.' In between, it is interesting to note the terms (social and interactive) which the parents used to express the improvement:

> *He doesn't just say one sentence, he makes it more meaningful.*
>
> *If she was asking a question, it used to be basic. Now it's longer and more of a conversation.*
>
> *He's listening more, joins in, speaks better.*

One parent reported the aspect most noted in the parental interviews by saying that her son now told her everything he had done during the day, whereas before he did not talk much. He was more confident, and this had been noticed also by the nursery staff.

On benefit to children's **reading** some parents recognised the problem of knowing if this often private activity had improved. As one parent said: 'He recognises a few more words, and enjoys it more − but he keeps it to himself.' However, there were some indirect examples of gain. The most frequently referred to was that children seemed to simulate the activity of reading more often. Some parents reported observable gain but, understandably, hesitantly:

> *She pretend reads to her sister.*
>
> *J is beginning to learn phonics.*
>
> *S can read now.*
>
> *The children see the time with (tutor's name) as exciting, ... fun.*

'His writing's getting better every week.' This activity is perhaps more observable than reading: respondents more easily identified development. Moreover, many parents had gained a clear view of the developmental importance of various pre-writing activities, and were able to state the developmental stage their child had reached, for example:

> *Both have learned to draw.*
>
> *A will sit painting.*
>
> *He's improved, his letters are improving, not just squiggles.*
>
> *N will try and write his name.*
>
> *His spelling is much better.*

It is not a coincidence that these comments echo the developmental scale for writing described above, since the concepts involved in 'emergent writing' were known to both the researcher who devised the scale and the teachers in the Programmes, and those teachers used them as part of the basis for sessions with parents on early literacy development.

There were many reports of increase both in children's willingness to write and in their confidence when they did so. On confidence, one parent cited her son's asking about things he didn't understand: 'Quite a hard thing to do. Nobody likes to admit defeat.'

When asked at the follow-ups if they thought their children were continuing to benefit from the Programmes, a majority of parents who were interviewed referred to their children's increased confidence in literacy. Many also mentioned their increased attainment in literacy.

6.6 Benefit to other children in the family

Informal observation of the crèches showed that the younger children were receiving care and nurturing of very high quality, and crèche workers were reported by coordinators as having noticed improvements in their charges. In interviews, parents were asked a standard question about benefit to other children, and this produced about 25 relevant comments. Almost all of these were very positive, as these representative quotations will show:

> *My daughter and I have enjoyed reading the stories my (older) son has written. He also enjoys looking at what I am doing at night for the course. At times he has even helped me through discussing aspects of the course. I've been able to find out just what he finds helpful with his reading and writing.*
>
> *When (older daughter) comes in from school she likes to be the teacher. She's recently brought a book home from school – they've been doing the words 'look' and 'here' – and she was getting (younger daughter) to repeat these words.*
>
> *I think (younger son) is really benefiting. When the girls are drawing or writing, I give him a piece of paper and some chunky crayons as well. He's getting loads out of the crèche as well. I think what I do at home with the girls will really pay off with him.*

6.7 Teachers' views on children from the Programmes

On the 13 children for whom information was returned, the teachers said their progress in speaking and writing was about average for pupils of that age in that class; for reading, average progress was perhaps slightly better. For all three aspects of language, the teachers' opinion was that that amount of progress was on average slightly better than they would have expected from their impressions of them early in the term.

During follow-up interviews, parents were asked if they had had any feedback from their child's teacher. Of 39 parents who had a child in school by this stage and who provided comments, only seven said they had had no feedback or a negative comment. From the remaining 32 positive comments, the following are some representative examples:

> *She says my son is really wonderful, he gives all. She couldn't ask for more.*
>
> *Our daughter has got a super teacher, she really is, but she seems to think she is making lots of progress. In her last class she had gone in being a real handful, and by the time she had come out of the other end it was said to us she had definitely made a great deal of progress.*
>
> *Since January the nursery teacher has said that his fine motor skills have noticeably improved. He writes over his name and has good control over his pencil. She says he loves drawing and looking at books.*
>
> *She's come on a lot better than before. She's more able to go and do things in class if you explain clearly to her. Mrs B. is very pleased with her. I should have brought her report to show you.*

In one area, two small confirmatory pieces of evidence became available. The educational psychologist who had worked with two of the Programme schools for some years said that she could see the improvement in the relevant children's abilities. And one of these schools had an OFSTED inspection in February 1995; the report included the following statement:

> *'A link with a local Family Literacy Initiative group has benefited children and their families.'*

6.8 Summary

- The children made **greater-than-expected average improvements in vocabulary during the courses and in the 12 weeks after them,** and made further, 'normal' progress in the next six months.

- In reading, they made **greater-than-expected average improvements during the courses and** (for two out of three relevant cohorts) in the 12 weeks after them, and made further, 'normal' progress in the next six months.

- In both vocabulary and reading, **the proportion of children who were severely disadvantaged for learning or struggling fell, and the number in the average or able range rose.** In particular,

- in vocabulary, at the beginning of the courses, the proportion of chldren who were severely disadvantaged for learning was 17 per cent; by the end of the courses, this had fallen to 10 per cent, and by the 12-week follow-up, to six per cent

- in reading, at the beginning of the courses, the proportion who were severely disadvantaged for learning was 24 per cent; by the end of the courses, this had fallen to 19 per cent, and by the 12-week follow-up, to nine per cent

- In writing, the children made substantial average improvements during the courses, and in the 12 weeks after them, and in the next six months. The evaluators' judgment was that all these improvements in writing were greater than the children would have made without the Programmes.

- Thus many children had benefited in all three aspects of language.

- The initiative was working for the great majority of children; a high proportion of them were better equipped for school learning as a direct result of the Programmes.

- But a minority had not made such good progress, and in vocabulary and reading were being left, relatively, further behind.

- Parents' views on their children's progress during and after the courses were strongly positive.

- The small amount of evidence available from the Programmes' host schools confirmed the findings from the quantitative data and the parents' opinions.

CHAPTER SEVEN

Parents' progress in ability to help their children

It would not have been practicable, or acceptable, to carry out observations in participating families' homes. Evidence for the impact of the initiative on parents' ability to help their children was therefore gathered indirectly, by:

- *asking parents on each occasion of testing to estimate, in an interview with their tutor during which a relevant questionnaire was completed, how often they carried out certain literacy-related activities with their children at home*

- *asking parents who were interviewed by the evaluators a small number of similar questions about the frequency of certain literacy activities, and about change in that frequency*

- *gathering parents' opinions in writing about the effect of the Programmes on the frequency of literacy-related activities with their children*

- *gathering parents' opinions about the effect of the Programmes on their ability to help their children; these opinions were gathered both in writing and during interviews.*

7.1 Literacy-related activities at home: the Home Activities questionnaire

On each occasion of testing parents were asked to complete, in an interview with their tutor, a questionnaire about literacy-related activities at home. The numbers of questionnaires returned are shown in Appendix A, section A.8, and the questionnaire itself is reproduced in Appendix B, together with the distribution of responses on all the items, summed across cohorts. A picture of literacy-related home activities before participation was given in section 5.4. This section is concerned with comparisons between the beginning of the course and later occasions.

Differences between the distributions of responses on the four occasions were analysed statistically. The points on the response scale were treated as though they were equal-interval ordinal values, and the arithmetic means were calculated on this basis. Then the significance of the differences was estimated by t-tests.

The statistical tests of the differences between the beginning and end of the courses revealed a significant increase ($p<0.05$) on every item. Inspection the data revealed that parents were reporting particularly substantial increases during the courses on the following items:

- looking at: magazines
               newspapers
               TV guides
               labels on food packets
               letters
- writing a shopping list
- the child writing his/her own name
- drawing/painting
- using a computer
- playing with make-believe toys
- cutting and sticking
- making a scrapbook

- talking about television
- children making up stories for parents
- playing schools
- singing songs
- telling nursery rhymes
- going on outings
- parents reading stories to children
- borrowing children's books from a library
- parents helping with school activities
- parents talking with the child's teacher.

Most of the items in this list were activities that the Programme staff had been encouraging and which were feasible for those with limited financial resources. Of the activities not showing much shift some (for instance looking at books, watching TV, talking about TV, child telling parent what happened at school) were already so frequent that little increase was possible.

In all cases, gains made during the course were at least sustained at both follow-ups. Between the end of the course and the 12-week follow-up, some activities showed a further increase:

- using a computer
- cutting and sticking

- making a scrapbook
- telling nursery rhymes,

and there was also a further significant increase in the average number of books children owned.

Similarly, between the two follow-ups further significant increases were reported in:

- writing shopping lists
- drawing/painting
- going on outings

- borrowing children's books from the library.

However, it was in this period that the only significant **decreases** occurred, in:

- looking at catalogues
- newspapers.

The general picture was that a wide range of literacy-related home activities increased during the courses, and became firmly embedded in family practice.

7.2 Literacy-related activities at home: the frequency questions asked by the evaluators

In order to gather an additional quantitative impression of the extent to which parents had increased the frequency of some literacy-related home activities with their children, parents who were **interviewed** during the courses were asked five questions about how frequently they had undertaken certain activities with their children before the course, and then whether they now engaged in those activities more or less frequently, or about as often. The questions, the distributions of responses to them, and the estimates of change are shown in Table 7.1.

Table 7.1: **Interviewed parents' estimates of frequency and change of literacy-related home activities**

In the last *week*, how many times has your child . . .	Frequency											Change		
	0	1	2	3	4	5	6	7	8	9	10+	+	=	−
seen you reading or writing?	1	2	8	16	12	9	13	32	3	6	9	68	41	2
shared a book with you?	0	2	9	12	10	12	13	41	2	3	7	70	36	5
asked you to read to him/her?	11	4	10	8	14	12	8	34	2	4	4	66	33	12
scribbled, printed, made letters, or written AT HOME?	0	0	5	6	17	15	10	32	2	7	17	74	34	3
In the last **month**, how many times have you taken your child to the library?	48	15	26	9	10	0	1	0	1	0	1	40	61	10

For all items, sample size = 111.

It seems likely that the high frequency of the response 'seven times a week' in the first four lines of Table 7.1 was a numerical translation of 'every day'.

More significant than the supposedly 'absolute' figures in any case were the data on change in frequency, which were consistent in suggesting a greater frequency overall, though of course not for every family. Moreover, in their general pattern these figures were also fully consistent with the data from the home activities questionnaire.

7.3 Literacy-related activities at home: parents' written opinions

One of the questions on which parents were asked to write at the end of the course was 'Have there been any changes in what you do at home with your children, whilst you have been on the course?'

The answers revealed that many parents (40 per cent) devoted substantially **more time to reading** with their children at home, and that some (17 per cent) also helped with **writing** or making books; but that in many cases (18 per cent) the amount of time spent **talking and listening** to their child had also increased.

While many parents referred to a greater emphasis on reading with their children, an equally large proportion (42 per cent) commented on the increase in the amount of **creative activity or play** that they arranged for or participated in with their child.

One in five parents (21 per cent) simply said they and their children now spent **more time together.**

Two representative quotations from what parents wrote at the end of the course are these:

> *I try to do a lot more with the children. We do more reading together, and also cooking and science experiments. We play more together also, doing jigsaws and playing games. I have a lot more patience with the children since being on the course.*
>
> *I read a lot more, make toys, play games. We have more of a laugh and we all enjoy talking about the work which we have done. The telly is on a lot less and we have all learned how to cooperate with each other.*

At the time of the **12-week follow-up,** parents noted **a continued increase** in the amount of time they spent **reading or sharing books** with their children (45 per cent) and also a substantial increase in the time they spent in **writing or book-making** with their children (25 per cent). In most other respects, the extent of the joint activities mentioned at the end of the course had been sustained.

Moreover, two items that had not figured in the written responses at the end of the courses now appeared. About one in eight (13 per cent) of the parents responding said that they now paid **regular visits to the library** with their children; about one in five (22 per cent) said that they arranged more **outings or activities outside the home** which sometimes involved the whole family.

Nine months after the course, the figures for **library visits and other outings had further increased**. At this stage about one in five of the parents (19 per cent) said that they arranged regular library visits, and one in four (26 per cent) made arrangements for outings and activities involving the children.

What parents wrote about their activities with their children was again fully consistent with the evidence already cited. Indeed, in respect of library visits and family outings the parents' written evidence suggested new features.

Moreover, the three sources of evidence agreed in implying that **parents' ability to help their children's language and literacy development had substantially increased**.

7.4 Parents' views on their ability to help their children

Evidence on this point was drawn from two of the questions on which parents were asked to write at the end of the course, namely '**Have there been any changes in what you do at home with your children, whilst you have been on the course?**' and '**What do you think you have gained from the course?**' In neither case were parents asked explicitly about their ability to help their children.

Many parents said that they had learnt how to **help their child learn to read** (22 per cent) **and to write** (16 per cent). Others said that they had learnt how to **help them play creatively** (16 per cent), through making games or toys, for example.

Over a third of the parents (37 per cent) mentioned that they had gained a **greater understanding of what children learn and how they are taught**.

Many parents referred to a **change in their relationship with their children** which was marked by growth in **patience** or mutual understanding. In fact, over one in five (21 per cent) of the parents felt that they had more **patience** with their child. This derived, some mentioned, from their deeper understanding of how children learn. Again two representative quotations from what parents wrote at the end of the course are these:

> *I have changed a lot at home with my attitude towards my child. I don't fob him off now when he wants my attention. I stop and listen to him more. I also do more activities at home with him at night times, like cutting things out and making things.*
>
> *There have been a lot of changes at home, because we are more confident and at ease with each other, we don't get so frustrated when working together, because I have the insight of how they are taught.*

These changes were in turn reflected in a development in the relationship of children and parents as regards teaching and learning. The children had discovered, or perhaps it would be more accurate to say had rediscovered, that their parents were able to teach them; and the parents had found that helping their child to learn in these ways was an enjoyable and rewarding experience. **It was as if an apparent barrier between home and school had been crossed.**

In the 12-week follow-up the parents' responses regarding the main gains from the course were generally similar to those given at the end of the course, but a number were even more positive. For example, a larger proportion appeared to be **more confident** than at the end of the course that they had the **knowledge to help their child to read** (26 per cent) **and to write** (20 per cent).

The parents' responses to the questions asked in the nine-month follow-up indicated that gains made were still evident in most respects. Generally, parents were **even more confident** than they were at the end of the course that they knew how to help their children **to read** (30 per cent) **and to write** (19 per cent); and a higher proportion said that they knew how to help their children to **play creatively** (16 per cent).

In **interviews during the courses**, all but a few parents agreed that they had learned things to help them help their children. Between half and two-thirds mentioned that they had learnt strategies for helping their children variously with reading, writing and talking. They had learnt both specific teaching skills, and the general attitude of patience. Among the specific skills, phonics was mentioned quite often. Many other skills relevant to fostering early reading and writing were mentioned. All of this showed, as one parent put it, 'A basic understanding about how reading and writing are taught.'

At the **12-week follow-up interview**, parents were asked specifically whether they had more confidence about helping their children, and whether they thought they knew more about how children learn to read and write.

Within these prompted responses, there were many references to gains of this sort; no parent denied any gain at all. There were only a few parents who qualified their responses in any way. These mainly seemed to indicate that they would like to receive further support, irrespective of the progress they could already identify. For example, one parent was 'still a bit confused' and 'would like to have done more' about how children learn. Another, as a result of diagnosis during the course, had received a document stating her educational needs on the grounds of her dyslexia. The course had nevertheless helped her to help her children; realistically and confidently, she could identify that help in terms of tips for a home reading session: pointing under words, left to right directionality, and having the reading book in the best position.

All the parents interviewed at the 12-week follow-up could identify ways in which their **greater understanding of reading and writing processes now helped them support their children's progress**. For the majority of these parents, knowledge and understanding gave them confidence to help their children. They appreciated the way in which their courses initiated them into some theoretical understanding of processes of reading and writing, but it was an acquaintance with the ways in which schools implement these processes, and an understanding of practical ways in which parents can help at home, that were most frequently mentioned. Parents appreciated, and were given confidence through, the following:

- *learning about different methods in different schools*

- *understanding about the importance of materials for support activities*

- *being helped to identify ways of introducing activities that support reading and writing into daily routines at home: shopping lists, labels, etc.*

- *knowing about what makes a productive home reading session (the three elements already mentioned by the dyslexic parent reported above, together with such things as using picture cues, word attack skills, and phonics).*

Parents also appreciated the opportunity to get the feel of the pace and style of the reading and writing support they could offer at home. At venues and on courses where there was sufficient room space and programme time, the **joint sessions** activities, pitched at a level appropriate to their own children, were reported as being useful – 'Through doing the course, I learned the best way to help her.'

It was probably from experience of these joint sessions that the parents picked up what several reported: their new understanding that reading development is more likely when reading is an activity frequently shared with a patient adult:

> *I didn't realise how difficult it was for children to learn to read from scratch. "You know it", I'd say.*

The dimension that parents referred to most frequently in the responses to these probes was a **new-found interaction and co-operation** with their children. The references were sometimes tangential, but always present: it was possible to infer parent-child interaction in the responses of every parent without exception. And many of the parents considered improving relationships with their children an important benefit – over half said this explicitly. Put together, a plaudit for the courses, and a possible explanation of why confidence seemed to burgeon: **the parents were beginning to enjoy their own success as they saw their children's progress.**

7.5 Summary

- Responses from a home activities questionnaire, from frequency questions asked during interviews with parents and from what parents wrote were fully consistent in suggesting **substantial increases in literacy-related home activities**, especially those carried out jointly by parents and children.

- Many of the increased activities related directly to literacy, for instance frequency of parent and child sharing a book.

- Many others related more directly to children's facility with speech, for instance discussing television programmes, creative play.

- In writing and interviews, **parents also reported substantial increases in their ability to help their children** with language and literacy and in their **confidence** in doing so.

- Also frequently cited was parents' feeling that their **relationship with their child had greatly improved**.

- Two overall conclusions emerged:
  - Parents seemed to feel that a barrier between school practice and home activities had been crossed, and
  - they were beginning to enjoy their own success as they saw their children's progress.

CHAPTER EIGHT

Parents' progress in literacy and other skills

8.1 Parents' reading attainment

The average scores on the three parts of the cloze test, on the basis of returners and summing across cohorts, were as shown in Table 8.1.

Table 8.1: **Parents' cloze test (reading) scores: returners only**

N	Mean scores (s.d's)			
	Beginning of course	**End of course**	**12-week follow-up**	**9-month follow-up**
	Part 1 (maximum = 11)			
209	8.8 (1.8)			
142	**8.9** (1.7)	**9.5** (1.3)		
80	8.7 (1.9)	**9.3** (1.4)	**9.8** (1.2)	
28	8.6 (2.3)	9.3 (1.3	**9.8** (1.3)	**9.5** (1.8)
	Part 2 (maximum = 17)			
257	12.6 (2.5)			
170	**12.8** (2.5)	**13.9** (1.9)		
91	12.8 (2.2)	**13.7** (1.9)	**13.7** (2.4)	
35	12.7 (2.3)	14.1 (1.7)	**13.3** (2.7)	**14.0** (2.6)
	Part 3 (maximum = 34)			
353	22.6 (4.8)			
282	**22.9** (4.6)	**24.6** (3.4)		
161	23.1 (4.6)	**24.9** (3.5)	**24.8** (3.4)	
55	23.5 (5.0)	25.2 (3.8)	**25.7** (4.1)	**24.8** (4.1)

Key: N = sample size; s.d. = standard deviation

The tendency for parents with lower early scores not to return is clear in the results for test 3 in the second column. That this tendency was not apparent for tests 1 and 2 may be due to these tests having been given only to parents who were less likely to be successful with test 3. The standard deviations showed no tendency to increase over time, and possibly a weak tendency to diminish; therefore parents with lower initial scores seem to have made the same amount of progress, relatively, as those with higher initial scores.

All the end of course means were significantly higher (p<0.05) than those for the beginning of the course; across the three tests, the improvement averaged five per cent of the maximum score. Therefore **the parents made substantial progress in reading during the courses,** and **this improvement can confidently be attributed to the Programmes,** since nothing else that was happening in the parents' lives at the time could account for it.

The difference between the 12-week follow-up and the end of course was significant for test 1, but not for test 2 or test 3. Therefore **some parents** (perhaps some of those with the poorest reading, since they were still being entered for test 1 at this stage) **continued to improve their reading immediately after the courses, while others sustained the improvement made during them.**

The differences between the 12-week and 9-month follow-ups were non-significant for all three tests. Therefore, again **the improvements made during the courses were sustained, and there was no statistical evidence of wash-out.**

The analysis by parents' qualifications for the end of the course continued to show that those with qualifications had significantly higher mean scores on all three parts of the test than those with none. At the follow-ups, the same tendency was apparent in the mean scores, but the numbers of parents in the two categories had fallen to the point where the differences were no longer statistically significant.

8.2 Parents' writing attainment: impression marks

Average scores for parents' writing were calculated by treating the general impression scores on the seven-point scale as equal-interval ordinal values. These averages, on the basis of returners and summing across cohorts, were as shown in Table 8.2.

As for reading, the standard deviations again showed no tendency to increase over time, and therefore parents with lower initial scores seem to have made the same amount of progress, relatively, as those with higher initial scores.

None of the differences in line 4 were significant; this may have been due to the relatively small number of parents who provided writing samples at the 9-month follow-up.

The difference between the scores for the end and the beginning of the courses in line 2 was significant, and the same was true for the corresponding difference in line 3; the improvement was about 10 per cent of the average starting score. This shows that **the parents concerned made good progress in writing during the courses**; and **this improvement also must be attributed to the Programmes.**

Table 8.2: **Average scores for parents' writing: returners only**

Mean scores (s.d's)				
N	Beginning of course	End of course	12-week follow-up	9-month follow-up
314	4.6 (1.3)			
251	**4.6** (1.3)	**5.1** (1.3)		
151	4.5 (1.3)	**5.0** (1.3)	**5.1** (1.3)	
56	4.4 (1.2)	5.2 (1.4)	**5.1** (1.3)	**5.5** (1.2)

Key: N = sample size; s.d. = standard deviation

The differences between the scores for the 12-week follow-up and the end of the courses, and between the two follow-ups, were non-significant. **The parents had sustained the improvement in writing they had achieved during the course**, and not slipped back.

The analysis of impression marks by parents' qualifications for the end of the course and the 12-week follow-up again showed that those with qualifications had a significantly higher mean score than those with none. At the 9-month follow-up, the same tendency was apparent in the mean scores, but the numbers of parents in the two categories had fallen to the point where the difference was no longer statistically significant.

What the cloze test data for parents' reading and the general impression data for their writing show is that **these parents had achieved substantial improvements in their literacy skills during the courses and maintained those improvements thereafter.**

8.3 Parents' writing attainment: analytic marks

During the courses, there was a significant increase in the length of parents' scripts, and in the number of parents whose handwriting was classified as falling into Category 3, that is handwriting which was legible and accurate in all major respects. However, there was no significant change in respect of the parents' knowledge of orthographic, grammatical or stylistic conventions in the course of the twelve-week programme.

71

At the 12-week follow-up, however, parents' control of grammatical conventions showed a significant improvement when compared to the beginning of the course. The improvement continued to be apparent in the 9-month follow-up assessment. At this point a significant improvement was also apparent in respect of the parents' knowledge of stylistic conventions.

There was a significant improvement also in the parents' knowledge of orthographic conventions between the two follow-up surveys. In the 12-week follow-up survey, the writing showed a mean of 2.1 errors per script. This had fallen to 1.2 errors per script for those involved in the 9-month follow-up study. At this point, also, virtually all those involved were assigned a handwriting score of 3, a significant improvement over the first follow-up study.

One measure of the improvements is the proportions of parents who made no errors in specific categories at the different stages of assessment: see Figure 8.1.

Figure 8.1: **Percentages of parents registering no errors in various writing assessment analytic categories, by occasion of testing**

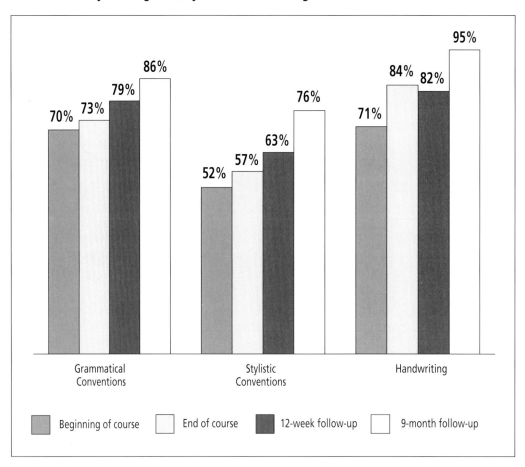

At the beginning of the course half of those responding (51 per cent) made no orthographic errors and the proportion was the same at the end of the course.

Parents tended to write longer scripts as time went by. In order to get an indication of the relative number of errors relating to grammar and style in relation to the amount written, an error/length ratio was calculated for each stage.
What this analysis showed was that there was little significant change between the beginning and end of the course. By the time of the 12-week follow-up, however, a reduction in the number of errors in relation to length was apparent, from 12.6 to 10.2 errors. By the time of the nine-month follow-up the error/length ratio had fallen even further, to 7.3, the difference between the two stages being significant.

In interpreting these findings, it should also be borne in mind that the content of the writing task parents undertook at the beginnng of the course was significantly less difficult than those undertaken on later occasions. In particular, a wider range of vocabulary was needed in writing about changes seen in their children and in their home activities at the end of the course (and later) than was needed for writing in general terms about their children at the start of the course.

To summarise, there were improvements:

- *during the course: in general impression, content, amount written and handwriting*

- *at the 12-week follow-up: in grammar and in a fall in the frequency of errors*

- *at the 9-month follow-up: in style, orthography and handwriting, and in a further fall in the frequency of errors.*

In this context, the fact that the parents' control of grammar, orthography and style improved significantly **after** the courses, but did not lead to a further significant improvement in overall scores, makes good sense. The most powerful correlates of overall scores for writing tend to be content and organisation, and length is in turn correlated with organisation. During the courses, therefore, the details of parents' writing improved in the ways which have the strongest impact on overall scores; and later, **continued** contact with the programme was associated with eventual improvement in the more linguistic aspects of writing. Thus in their greater control of the **formal features** of writing, the parents' perseverance did produce results.

8.4 Accreditation of parents' literacy and other achievements

In addition to their literacy gains, virtually all the parents involved achieved wider recognition of their literacy and other achievements. Information supplied by the

Programmes showed that, across the four Programmes and the five terms from Spring 1994 to Summer 1995, **95 per cent of all the parents who enrolled attained partial or full accreditation of a level of Wordpower.**

(In some cases, the Adult Basic Skills teachers deliberately arranged that parents would not quite have finished a level of Wordpower at the end of the course, so that parents would have a more powerful incentive to go on to another course.)

All four Programmes also ensured that parents achieved other forms of accreditation:

- *in one area, 85 per cent of parents achieved accreditation in word-processing*

- *in another, all those achieving some accreditation on Wordpower also achieved it in 'Understanding How Children Learn'*

- *in the remaining two, the other certificate obtained was in First Aid, 97 per cent in one area, 100 per cent in the other.*

Also, all parents received certificates celebrating their achievements. These were usually presented at a specially arranged ceremony the following term, and by a local councillor or other well-known person. At one such ceremony which was observed by a fieldworker, the pride the parents took in the public recognition of their achievements was plain to see.

8.5 Parents' views on their own progress in literacy

The first question on which parents were asked to write at the end of the course was **'What do you think you have gained from the course?'** The question did not refer explicitly to literacy, and most responses were on other topics. However, many parents did write about gains in their **literacy** attainments, and the great majority of these (29 per cent) referred to **knowledge about writing**, in particular the writing of letters. Over one in five (22 per cent) expressed appreciation of the exposure they had had to computers and, more particularly, to **word-processing**.

At the 12-week follow-up, these responses were maintained, and at the nine-month follow-up 10 per cent felt that their own **writing proficiency had continued to improve.**

The benefits to their own literacy to which parents made most references in **interviews** during the course are summarised in Table 8.3.

Table 8.3: **Literacy benefits to themselves identified by parents in interviews during courses**

Cohort	Summer 1994	Autumn 1994	Spring 1995	Summer 1995	Total
Number of respondents	32	39	35	17	123
Number of references					
Reading improved	6	5	12	10	33
Writing improved	20	26	30	19	95
Computing and word-processing	14	28	21	18	81
Letterwriting	9	35	23	24	91

Only one parent (from all the groups) was not prepared to recognise any benefit. She said, 'I was a good reader, anyway'.

Every parent interviewed at the 12-week follow-up claimed that they were continuing to benefit from the course after it had finished. One of the two items most frequently mentioned was improvements in their reading and writing (the other being confidence in their own abilities – see below). At the 9-month follow-up the pattern was very similar.

8.6 Parents' views on their own social skills

Writing at the end of the course on what they had gained from it, over half (52 per cent) of the parents responding referred to a growth in their **confidence**. Often the answers referred to the contexts in which this was apparent. They felt, for example, more confident in their own literacy, in talking to a group of people, in talking to teachers, or in directing their own children's learning. In one Programme, two parents planned to give talks to their group lasting five minutes apiece; each lasted an hour.

A number of those responding commented on the fact that the course had also helped them to communicate with adults who, in many cases, had become their friends. The enjoyment they had in the company of their friends on the course was frequently referred to (by 15 per cent of respondents). It is apparent from the written comments made that almost all the parents had enjoyed the course and felt that they had benefited from it.

In the 12-week follow-up survey the parents' responses regarding the main gains from the course were generally similar to those given at the end of the course, and a number were even more positive. For example, a larger proportion (20 per cent) now said that they had made new friends. Some (seven per cent) also felt that they had become better at communicating with others, including their children, and others said that they were better at speaking in public and taking part in group discussion (five per cent).

The parents' responses in the nine-month follow-up indicated that the gains made were still evident in most respects, and in some had increased even further. For example, nearly a third (31 per cent) said that they had made new friends. This proportion was twice as high as at the end of the course.

All the parents **interviewed** during the courses (where there was need for them to become more confident) were able to identify gains in confidence in their own literacy. Also, references to confidence and/or to writing development were often associated with progress in word-processing. It is possible that where parents had little knowledge of computers, and a consequent fear of them, the initial rate at which they realised just how easy and useful they can be, and the amount of improvement in presentation they can engender, was itself a boost to their confidence.

Many parents emphasised the boost which the Programmes had given to their social skills. Of the 54 references to 'confidence' in interviews during the course, many were to increased confidence in social situations and with their children's teachers, as well as in their group. These interviews also contained 78 references to the social sharing, the learning from each other, that had been a positive feature of the courses. A frequent theme was expressed by the parent who said: '**We all had ideas and passed them round to help each other.**'

On what had actually been learnt from other parents, there were many references to picking up different approaches to children's development, and some to swapping ideas, learning about different activities, working together and gaining confidence from being with others. One parent had obviously experienced competition and failure in her own schooldays: she liked the co-operation of the Programme and the way her peers helped; she had felt on her own as a child, whilst at school, and often had not gone. Another parent pointed to a positive outcome of group co-operation: 'We now all talk about each other's kids. **We're not competing. We are all a group helping together.**'

The social benefits continued to be a theme in the follow-up interviews.

8.7 Parents' involvement with their children's schools

Three questions relevant to this topic were asked in the Home Activities questionnaire, and the distribution of responses can be found in Appendix B. The proportion of parents **attending school activities** and the average frequency of **talking to the child's teacher** both increased very substantially during the courses, and the proportion **helping with school activities** also increased significantly. The end-of-course increases were fully sustained at both follow-ups. Thus these parents continued to be more involved with their children's schools than the generality of parents in their circumstances.

These findings received small-scale confirmation from the teachers' impressions: from the 13 families, nine sets of parents had been in contact with school more than the teachers would have expected. Also, coordinators reported good feedback from host schools on parents' increased involvement. There were occasional reports of previously reluctant teachers now letting Family Literacy parents in to help in the classroom.

In written responses at the end of the course, few parents mentioned increased involvement with their children's schools, understandably since they had been busy with the course. However, in the 12-week follow-up some (four per cent) said that they had started to help in school more generally, not just in contact with their own children. And by the nine-month follow-up, the proportion of parents who were helping out in school (14 per cent) had increased substantially.

Similar evidence came from the **interviews** with parents. At the 9-month follow-up, 40 parents were asked the question 'And since our discussion six months ago, to what extent have you been involved in your child's school?' Of the 27 parents who said they were involved in some way, four had 'standard' involvement (such as parents' evenings, assemblies), eight had rather more regular contact (also going on school trips, for example), and the remaining 15 gave their children's schools regular practical support at least once a week. Details can best be given in their own words:

> *I help out once a week in the classroom, and work in the tuckshop every day.*
>
> *I'm involved quite a bit, because my son's having an educational assessment done at the moment. I link up with the headteacher and nursery staff to discuss his needs. We are all of the opinion that he should stay in the school with speech support.*
>
> *I do the crisps every morning, which gives me a lot of contact with the children and teachers. I go on the trips, and generally help out where needed.*
>
> *I've been helping with the nursery on a Wednesday morning, and helping with the packs (learning packs that children take home each week).*
>
> *I come in to hear the small ones read once a week and I enjoy that.*

Bynner and Steedman (1995) found that their parents' involvement in school had been one of the better predictors of the attainment of the cohort they had studied who had been born in 1970. The increased involvement of the parents in this study should therefore bode well for their children.

8.8 Destinations: parents' plans and how they worked out

In **interviews** during the course, parents were asked what their plans were. In general, they had quite definite plans, and these are summarised in Table 8.4.

Table 8.4: **Parents' plans at the end of the courses**

Cohort	Summer 1994	Autumn 1994	Spring 1995	Summer 1995	Total
Number of respondents	18	39	35	17	109
Number of references					
No plans indicated	1	3	2	1	7
Specified study	8	19	19	9	55
Unspecified study	9	12	10	5	36
General plans	1	4	5	8	18
Work	0	3	7	4	14
Maintaining the group	7	1	1	3	12
Baby care	0	2	0	0	2

Table 8.4 shows that nearly all parents had made some plans, mostly (more than 80 per cent) relating to a form of study, usually one which they could specify, often with some career or return to work intention. Less than seven per cent had not thought about future plans.

Table 8.5 extends the evidence of the one above. It presents information derived from interviews conducted 12 weeks after the course with 81 of the 92 respondents from the first three cohorts. Parents were asked whether they had planned to take another course when the Programme ended and how those plans had worked out.

Table 8.5: **Parents' intentions to take courses, and how they had worked out**

Cohort	Summer 1994	Autumn 1994	Spring 1995	Total
Number of respondents	24	32	25	81
Number of references				
Parents who had planned to take a course:	19	29	17	65
Of those, number actually taking a course:	12	25	15	52
Parents who had not planned to take a course:	5	1	8	14
Of those, number nevertheless taking one:	3	1	1	5
% taking a course:	61%	77%	64%	70%

Again, a very high take-up of courses was indicated, with only a fifth of those who had planned one not doing so, and 70 per cent overall taking a course. Some of the parents who were not currently taking a course explained that they wanted to, but that there were no vacancies on the one they wanted to do, or no crèche was available, or (occasionally) no suitable courses were available locally.

It should be remembered that the great majority of the parents who participated in the Programmes and went on to further courses were mothers. One unforeseen and unintended benefit of the Programmes, therefore, was that they had acted as **women's access courses.**

8.9 Summary

- During the courses, **the parents improved their average reading test scores by about five per cent** of the maximum on the tests.

- During the courses, **the parents improved their average writing score by about 10 per cent** of the starting level.

- **Both improvements were sustained** at both follow-ups.

- **95 per cent of all the parents who enrolled attained partial or full accreditation of a level of Wordpower.**

- Almost all parents also achieved accreditation of another skill developed during the course.

- Both in writing and in interviews parents confirmed the improvements in their literacy found on the tests.

- Over half (52 per cent) of the parents responding also referred to a growth in their **confidence**, and many reported other improvements in social skills.

- **The number of parents actively involved in their children's schools increased significantly.**

- At the end of the course, **over 80 per cent of parents planned to go on studying,** and 12 weeks **after the courses 70 per cent were actually doing a further course.**

- The Programmes had acted as **women's access courses.**

CHAPTER NINE

Why were the Programmes successful?
(1) Human factors in the process

9.1 Introduction

There were many factors which, in the evaluators' judgement, contributed to the effectiveness of the Programmes. An attempt will be made in this chapter and the next to tease out a fairly large number of those factors. Moreover, a suggested distinction will be drawn between:

> • *factors which appeared to be crucial in the **process** of achieving success; most of these are 'human', in a broad sense, and they will be dealt with in this chapter*

> • *factors which appeared to be preconditions or **prerequisites** for success; most of these are 'material', again in a broad sense, and they will be dealt with in chapter 10.*

9.2 Clear aims and objectives

Unclear or conflicting aims rarely create success, and more often ensure failure. The aims of this initiative were very clear from the start, and were expressed in a precise model, or set of guidelines (see chapter 2). These were the basis of the specification from the Agency to the Programmes. The aims were also fully consistent with each other, and created a coherent, interlocking whole.

Two aspects of the clarity of the aims need to be singled out. First, the aims were realistic and attainable, and did not (as in some US programmes) over-reach themselves by seeking to effect significant social and/or employment success for participants. Secondly, the linguistic aims were not (again as in some US programmes) too narrowly focused on reading alone, but took in talking and writing also.

9.3 Careful selection of Programmes

The selection by the Agency of areas to host the Demonstration Programmes was done from detailed knowledge of them, and from a history of fruitful collaboration between those chosen and the Agency. This avoided a possibly long and cumbersome application and screening process, and ensured that from the outset the Agency was working with local line managers and other partners who already understood the Agency's aims and methods. The local partners therefore saw the need for, and provided, the material prerequisites for the Programmes' success (for these, see the next chapter). They also understood that the Programmes' intergenerational nature required joint staffing by Adult Basic Skills and Early Years teachers (and crèche staff), in order to ensure the appropriate mix of talents and experience; and these requirements were met.

9.4 Careful selection of teachers

Many of the Early Years assistants were newly qualified, or trainees. Otherwise, all staff (Adult Basic Skills, Early Years and crèche) were highly qualified and experienced. From informal discussions with Line Managers and Agency staff it was clear that Programme staff were very carefully selected. The already close relationship between the Agency and its partners in the chosen areas meant that, right at the start, there were Adult Basic Skills and Early Years teachers in the Programmes who were highly experienced and ready to take the initiative on board.

In the four terms of the evaluation, involving between 20 and 30 Adult Basic Skills and Early Years teachers in all, only one appointment proved unsatisfactory.

Not all staff were paid employees; all the Programmes benefited to some extent from the help of volunteers. One Adult Basic Skills Coordinator spoke for all when she stressed how valuable this had been, and how her Programme could not have operated without the volunteers. Two of the joint sessions observed included activities led by volunteers, very expertly.

The quality of the teachers in these Programmes can be described best in the parents' voices; see the views presented in Box 4. The opinions given there were all those written by one group in one Programme at the end of their course. The views could be matched for other terms and the other Programmes, and the evaluators came to share this admiration for the teachers.

An aspect of the teachers' skill that would not perhaps have been so obvious to the parents was their **adaptability**. In one Programme, the crèche organiser acted as nursery assistant for one group for one term, while her fellow crèche worker acted as crèche organiser, and the nursery assistant as crèche assistant. In another Programme, the Early Years Coordinator acted as Adult Basic Skills teacher to one group. Across Programmes there were several occasions when either an Adult Basic Skills or an Early Years teacher led a joint session alone, while her colleague deputised for an absent crèche worker. In all cases, the staff were fully qualified to take on the additional role, and were broadening their experience by doing so.

Box 4: Some parents' views on their teachers

The work has been easy to understand because of the way (teacher's name) has put it across, it's been made easy. If we are stuck, (teacher's name) has always been there.

No problems, (teacher's name) has made it fun. She's teaching you but it's not a set routine. At first I thought it might be a bit tedious but it has been fun and enjoyable.

I feel (teacher's name) is very understanding which helps when something unavoidable crops up. If there are any problems, (teacher's name) is always on hand to help.

I have had no problems with what has been taught. (Teacher's Name) makes her 'teachering' like a friend and explains everything. It has all been very well organised. I feel that ours is quite a lively group. There's a lot of fun in it. I really enjoy it and look forward to Monday morning.

I would have liked the sessions to go on longer but the times have fitted in well with my work commitments. I feel the sessions are flexible enough that they can be changed if anyone has a problem. (Teacher's name) is also flexible and very helpful. You don't realise you're getting taught.

Sometimes I've found things a bit of a rush at lunchtimes but no real problems. If anyone is unsure of something they can always approach (teacher's name), and you don't feel stupid.

The timing of the sessions has not been a problem (one full day and one half day). It's very easy going, and I feel (teacher's name) is very approachable. She doesn't make you feel as if you're stupid.

I think (teacher's name) has been really good at explaining everything. If anyone has trouble (teacher's name) is always there to help.

Help is always available. It's been very good, I'll be quite sorry when it finishes actually.

Help is always there if you get stuck.

The teachers from both backgrounds needed to be able to see the implications of the Agency's model, and operate it. Two features of the model in particular had strong implications for their work, namely its **intergenerational nature** and the **fixed time** available. These created the need for careful, detailed **joint planning**, and for making **best use of every teaching minute**.

9.5 Joint planning

The intergenerational nature of the Agency's model required that both the Adult Basic Skills and Early Years teachers should be experts in their own fields. All the coordinators stated that this was a crucial factor, and were often loud in praise of their colleagues. All coordinators testified to the benefit of the joint training sessions provided by the Agency.

One Adult Basic Skills Coordinator said that the preparatory term (Autumn term 1993 for three of the Programmes, Spring term 1994 for the fourth) had been valuable and essential for melding the Adult Basic Skills and Early Years Coordinators into a team.

An Early Years Coordinator said she and her Adult Basic Skills colleagues had good comradeship and were able to talk things through; everyone was flexible and this worked – it would not have if anyone had been stubborn.

One of her Adult Basic Skills colleagues confirmed the good working relationship. They fed off each other and had a similar approach, for example in being willing to let control go to the parents, and not needing to direct them all the time. They were careful about how they set up joint activities and about monitoring them while in progress.

Some points for joint decision were small, e.g. whether all teachers should be addressed by their first name (as is usual in Adult Basic Skills) or by title and surname (as in most primary schools). Some Programmes began with a distinction (first name for Adult Basic Skills tutors, title and surname for Early Years), but this could not be maintained, since parents wanted to address Early Years teachers by their first names. All Programmes eventually standardised on first names for everyone; the making of the decision was in itself a lesson in linguistic nicety.

A larger need for collaboration was pointed out by an Adult Basic Skills Coordinator: **the Early Years workers knew less about Wordpower and Adult Basic Skills tutors less about the national curriculum.** Both sides needed time to adjust to the other's professional ways. This coordinator felt that training for such Programmes should encompass this, as 'it would be nice to see both sides of the coin and it would help people to relate better to each other and appreciate the demands'. These demands in both cases focused on language development and teaching.

The quality of the planning can be seen in the timetables reproduced in chapter 3.

What both those timetables showed was that the requirements of the specification, including in particular accreditation through Wordpower, had been taken on board. What they also showed was that:

> • *working to a model had by no means produced uniformity; the timetables showed sensitive adaptation to local circumstances and needs*

> • *good use was to be made of every session*

> • *the planning had incorporated the multiple aims of the initiative; every parents' session had objectives both for the parents' own literacy and for their learning to help their children's language and literacy development, and was intended to dovetail with the following joint session.*

9.6 What the parents brought to the courses

However good the teachers and their planning, their teaching would have had less effect if the parents who participated had not brought both high aspirations and great commitment to the courses.

(i) Parents' aspirations for themselves and their children

Section 5.2 summarised these. It can be inferred that these parents brought strong, if nervous, expectations to their participation, and that this motivation was a significant factor in their own and their children's success.

(ii) Parents' literacy skills

The parents' levels of literacy were summarised in section 5.3. A few parents had very low levels of skills, and the great majority had low levels. They had therefore set themselves a hard challenge by enrolling.

(iii) Parents' commitment

The parents' commitment to the courses was shown in several ways:

> • *by the fact that they were all volunteers*
>
> • *in the initial courage needed to enrol*
>
> • *in high attendance, retention and accreditation rates*
>
> • *in the high proportions who returned to be tested at the end of the course*
>
> • *in what they said and wrote about their aspirations and concerns*
>
> • *in negotiating parts of the course content*
>
> • *in keeping their own accreditation records*
>
> • *in the extra time they put in outside classes, and*
>
> • *in the reported increases in literacy-related activities with their children.*

Recognition of what parents brought to the courses was part of the teachers' learning. In an early interview, an Adult Basic Skills Coordinator commented that she had thought that the parents who would be recruited would benefit from ideas of what to do about literacy with their children, but she was now much more aware of how much the parents already did. Similarly, an Early Years Coordinator said she had moved her own perception of her role; she had realised how little she had previously acknowledged the 'home curriculum' and its strengths.

9.7 The parents' focus

What the parents' aspirations and commitment meant was that from the start their motivation to succeed, both for themselves and with and for their children, was very high. Therefore, when they encountered:

- *highly experienced teachers with a clear aim and programme*

- *a clear objective for their children in terms of language development and emerging literacy, stated in the recruitment details,*

- *a clear objective for improving their ability to help their children, also stated in the recruitment details, and*

- *a clear specification of objectives for themselves, in the form of accreditation for Wordpower,*

they were able to sense at once both that their expectations could be met, and that achieving them within the **fixed time** available would require constant attendance and effort. The high attendance, retention and accreditation rates, and the gains achieved, all make it clear that the parents gave the courses great focus and concentration.

Two comments from interviews with parents will illustrate the point:

> *The timetable's been no problem. Some weeks there's been a lot of work but I've enjoyed doing it. It's always been like fun not work.*
>
> *I've been coming in an extra day to catch up on work. To be quite honest I've caught up now and I'm still coming in, so it was just probably an excuse at first.*

9.8 Group cohesion

However good their **individual** commitment and dedication to the courses, it is unlikely that the parents would have made such gains if their groups had not 'gelled'.

There were few reports of groups not gelling, and very few (two or three) of individuals not fitting in or making their presence irksome to others. In one parents' session that was observed, it was clear that the rest of the parents were taking great pains to 'work round' one who was (inappropriately) attempting to take a leading role. By contrast, the major impression from what the parents wrote at the end of the courses was that the groups worked very well, people were very collaborative, and they benefited greatly from each other and from the experience of working together. Box 5 presents some representative parts of this evidence.

Box 5: Parents' written testimony on group cohesion

The course also meant that I would get to know other mothers and I liked the way we were in a group and that we all were involved. At first I thought it would be like school, but it was the complete opposite, e.g. the fact that we were treated like adults. I gained a lot of confidence working with the other mothers and not just talking to them outside the school gates. Actually, working with them gave me a lot of confidence.

I also enjoyed mixing with other members of the group who have children of similar age and slightly older, and exchanging ideas and experiences with them.

It's a good way of meeting other parents with small children. As the children were all different ages, we all seemed to discuss how to help them the best way with maybe starting to read. Everybody had some very good ideas. As a parent I think it opened my eyes to all the different ways we can help our children to read and write and doing everyday things.

The story from interviews during the courses was very similar, as the quotations in Box 6 show.

Box 6: Parents' spoken testimony on group cohesion

Once I got over the shock, it was great and I wouldn't change anything. It was just at first. I was frightened of getting things wrong, and making a fool of myself. But after the fourth week, I thought no-one was bothered about what we couldn't do – we were all in it together.

I feel the company of the other parents is very helpful. It is good to know that everybody else is going through what you're going through.

I enjoyed the company, and I'd recommend it to anyone. Everyone was so friendly . . . it wasn't all talk about children on Wednesdays – it was for us.

It takes you out of yourself. I used to be shy. I didn't know anyone, I didn't talk to anyone before I started this.

The follow-up interviews provided evidence that members of some groups had stayed together, continued to support each other and gained as a result:

> *I made friends on the programme. We sort of cling together outside the school and do lots of things together. I have more confidence in my own ability.*

It was clear that some parents would not have stayed without the peer co-operation that they discovered. And this co-operation became a great aid to their learning.

But how was this learning encouraged by the teaching? This is explored in the next four sections, which comment on aspects of the quality of the teaching.

9.9 The quality of the teaching

Many of the characteristics which made the teaching so effective have already been implied in this chapter or chapter 3, but should now be summarised:

- *careful, precise planning for the fixed time available*

- *sensitivity to parents' and children's needs*

- *close collaboration between Adult Basic Skills and Early Years teachers*

- *a range of appropriate activities and teaching approaches*

- *keeping sessions on track*

- *effective use of time*

- *predominant stress on language development, not just in reading but also in writing and talking*

- *the genuinely intergenerational nature of the teaching provided; that is, there was excellent teaching for parents on their own, for children on their own, and then for parents and children together*

- *dovetailing of aims for parents', children's and joint sessions.*

In addition to these features, three more deserve to be analysed in greater depth: the teachers' flexibility in adapting plans to meet the parents' wishes; the efforts the teachers made to suit their teaching to the needs of individual parents and children; and their concomitant ability to reflect on their work, and thus adapt and improve it.

9.10 The teachers' responsiveness to the parents' agenda

An issue that arose for the evaluators in parents' sessions was the balance between the teachers' and the parents' agendas. On the one hand, teachers were prone to say that they followed the parents' wishes, but on the other it was clear that the Agency's model set definite expectations for content, via the specification of Wordpower accreditation. As the Adult Basic Skills Coordinator in one Programme put it:

> *The approach is the same as in any adult basic education, negotiated with students and flexible. It involves perhaps more input from the teachers than in other adult basic education, because all the students are coming for the same reason, i.e. their children. Also we've got to get through a great deal within 12 weeks, and we are consciously working on group skills. As for the content, we assume that the students will want to cover emergent writing, early reading, and their own progression onto other courses, but everything else comes out of their needs. We offer options (such as First Aid, which is always taken up). We intend to work on things that the parents feel they missed out on at school and need now.*

The truth appeared to be that the general framework was set by the Agency's model, and within that there was considerable flexibility to take account of parents' wishes, both on timetabling and on content. For example, one of the timetables reproduced in chapter 3 shows a week when parents chose the topic. Within the 18 parents' sessions observed there were two instances of this, both on spelling (but in different Programmes).

A detailed example of the flexibility that the teachers showed in meeting the parents' needs was mentioned by a parent in an interview. She sometimes had difficulty going to a particular session on her own course, but was then able to attend the corresponding session on the other course being run at the same site that term on different days.

9.11 Individualisation of teaching

The parents who participated varied in age, gender, confidence, qualifications and capability, and brought to the courses one or two sons or daughters aged between 3 and 6, who might be at home or in nursery or infant school, and might have social and/or educational difficulties, or neither. Such diversity required very capable organisation. Some idea has already been given (in chapter 3) of how Adult Basic Skills teachers coped with the diversity in parent groups by giving appropriate individual attention. This is also clear in what parents wrote and said about the teachers.

The need for individualisation was even greater in children's (and therefore joint) sessions, because of the rapidity of physical, linguistic and all other aspects of development between 3 and 7, and the profound qualitative differences in cognition between even 'average' 3- and 6-year-olds, not to speak of the extremes. Again, there was ample evidence from interviews with parents and coordinators that this challenge was successfully met in the great majority of sessions. In just one group, a couple of parents complained that some of the joint activities were pitched at the wrong level for their children, who were the only Year 1 children in a group otherwise consisting entirely of 3- and 4-year-olds:

> *I did not enjoy the joint sessions, not because I did not want to work with (child's name), but because I felt the activities were more geared towards younger children. I tend to think she gets bored . . . When they all get together, they tend to run around and she sees them doing it so she thinks she can. It was quite a large group for the joint sessions.*
>
> *I thought they should maybe change the activities a bit so the older ones did not get bored.*

There were very few comments of this sort; in general the mix of activities in children's sessions was such that children of all the ages involved were suited, and the joint activities could be adapted to take account of ages and stages of development.

An Early Years Coordinator said that, because of the small numbers of children, they were able to be very individual in what they did. She made an assessment, and asked the teachers for one, right at the start; then she worked individually with each of the children. At one site, some children had very poor skills, so she was working on very basic levels of literacy – letter recognition, phonics, early core vocabulary. 'Basically it's all the things that the school are doing and I am reinforcing for them.' With the nursery children she was doing basic language extension; among the reception-age children there was one who was very bright, with better skills than all those from Year 1, so she was working at the child's level. At the other site, none of the children were independent writers. Until she had helped them with the very basic skills she could not start on reading. She was hoping that her input would help them to move further towards that, 'but there won't be big leaps and bounds; it's a slow process'.

9.12 Reflective teaching

Another aspect of the teachers' skills that led to their success was their reflective attitude to their teaching. The close collaboration between Adult Basic Skills and Early Years teachers has already been noted; in addition, teachers were individually thoughtful about their own teaching.

For example, an Early Years Coordinator, interviewed in the Autumn term 1994, said that during the year stories and story-telling had become more dominant in her teaching. She was also trying out sequencing activities with the children at the beginning and end of the course, and comparing three-year-olds' and six-year-olds' interpretation of stories. She felt something further needed to be done about joint activities; what was being done was perhaps not all that could be. Timing was not always right; the previous day's session on parents and children watching television together had not been entirely liked by parents because it came so late in the course. And the short timescale of the courses meant that teachers never had a long clear run at anything, leaving it feeling somewhat 'bitty'.

Interviewed in the same term, the Adult Basic Skills Coordinator in another Programme said she and her Early Years colleague had looked at the areas of early literacy they wanted to cover, and how they saw this being done, and concluded that 'it was very prescriptive'. That term new teachers had come into the Programme, and obviously they had ideas of their own, so although the themes remained the same 'what we do around that theme might be slightly different'. Each week they did two joint sessions, and even though they planned them simultaneously 'it might be the same joint session but they are entirely different'.

The following term the same coordinator said of her parents' groups: 'Last term's was very noisy, but this term's is quieter. I've decided to do letter writing towards the end of the course because so many of them are gaining employment. I try to bring something fresh to each session and adapt to the needs of the particular group.'

The teachers were constantly revising their approach in this way, in the light of their experience.

9.13 The boost to parents' confidence

In chapter 8, one of the strongest findings that emerged was the huge boost that parents' confidence had received during the courses. This permeated all their comments; they felt more confidence in:

- *their own literacy*

- *their social skills*

- *their dealings with their children's schools*

- *their knowledge about how children learn, especially in reading and writing*

> • *their relationship with their children, especially in terms of patience and of fostering a teaching/learning atmosphere*

> • *their ability to help their children.*

This growth in parents' confidence was both an outcome of the courses, and a key human factor in the process of achieving the quantitative gains, for both parents and children.

9.14 Immediate practice in joint sessions

In the joint sessions, everything came together.

The aims of the initiative balanced benefit for parents and benefit for children, and envisaged that improving parents' own skills and their ability to help, and confidence in helping, their children's language and literacy would be one of the major mechanisms in producing benefit for children. The range of activities and teaching approaches in joint sessions was described in chapter 3; the quantitative and other evidence for increases in literacy-related activities was summarised in chapter 7; and two aspects of the effectiveness of the joint sessions (focus on language development; dovetailing of objectives for parents and children) were described earlier in this chapter.

Here the focus is on the way in which the joint sessions provided parents with the immediate chance to try out with their children what they had been learning. It may seem obvious that not to have had joint sessions would have been to waste a golden opportunity – but this is wisdom after the event, and the fact is that many schemes to which the label 'family literacy' is applied simply encourage parental involvement in reading, and provide no sessions in which parents can try out even that, still less receive feedback and encouragement. This was the most distinctive feature of these Programmes, and one quarter of the time on the courses was therefore given over to the joint sessions.

Those sessions were highly valued by the parents; some representative views were these:

> *We talked about the pictures and what was going on, although with (child's name) being a good reader, he was more keen to read the words. If he read a word wrong, he would go back to the beginning of the sentence and read it again. I felt the course had reinforced what I was doing with him at home.*

> *I encouraged them more to talk and to describe things to extend their vocabulary. The joint sessions have helped with this. Now, for example, when getting things out of the washing basket we talk more about each item, colour, shape, who it belongs to, etc.*
>
> *I know now a lot more about children's learning and what it's like to start school. When my child starts reception in September I feel that I'll know what he will be doing and that I can help him more. With all the activities I feel that I play and work with him more.*

The coordinators also emphasised the value to parents of being able to move with little delay (and often directly) from a separate session in which they learnt an activity they could use with their children to a joint session in which they could try it out. Moreover, the presence of both Adult Basic Skills and Early Years teachers in the joint session meant that parents could have prompt feedback on their use of the activity, in the confidence that their performance would be sympathetically and accurately evaluated for them; they could also, in appropriate circumstances, have the parent's role modelled for them by a teacher.

What this immediate practice gave rise to for the parents was an **evident delight in their success in helping their children**, reinforced by seeing the progress in language that the children were making, thus **completing the virtuous circle** from the parents' aspirations for themselves and their children, through the teaching and learning, back to the **clear consciousness of having achieved great and demonstrable progress in language** within a strictly limited time.

9.15 International comparisons

In Britain, the Family Literacy programme is unique; it is the only two-generation, three-pronged initiative. For comparisons with sufficiently similar programmes it is therefore necessary to look abroad; in fact, to the United States, where the only comparable programmes which have been the subject of adequately designed quantitative evaluations were based. St. Pierre *et al.* (1994) analysed the results of the seven such evaluations, and reached the overall conclusion that the evidence on their effectiveness was mixed:

- *'As they are currently designed, two-generation programs have small or no short-term effects on a wide set of measures of child development.*

- *Two-generation programs have scattered short-term effects on measures of parenting . . .*

> • *Two-generation programs have large short-term effects on attainment of a GED (General Education Diploma), but these are not accompanied by effects on tests of adult literacy . . .*

> • *Where we find positive effects, those effects are generally small . . .'* (St. Pierre *et al.*, 1994, p.18)

It is argued in Appendix A that the PPVT results from the United States reported in chapter 6 are more reliable than St. Pierre *et al.* allow, but this would make little difference to the strength of their conclusion, and the Agency's Family Literacy Programmes were clearly more effective than this. It was the present evaluators' judgement that certain systematic differences between the Agency's Programmes and those in the United States were crucial to the difference in effectiveness. These differences were that:

> • *some programmes in the US had grandiose social and socioeconomic aims; the Family Literacy Programmes avoided these and focused clearly on literacy and language development of parents and children, treating any other effects as bonuses*

> • *many programmes in the US concentrate on reading; the Family Literacy Programmes avoided this, and genuinely focused also on talking and writing*

> • *in some US programmes, participation is linked with entitlement to social security benefits; in the Family Literacy Programmes, all participating parents were volunteers*

> • *in many US programmes (as in almost all Adult Basic Skills courses in Britain) there is no time limit, and students may stay on a course as long as they like, and participate intermittently; in the Family Literacy Programmes, the fixed time limit concentrated all minds, and the attendance rate was very high – over 90 per cent on all courses*

> • *in some US programmes, the intergenerational aspect is not strong – the focus may be on children, with parents attending but not actively participating, or the focus may be on parents, with children cared for but not taught; by contrast, the Family Literacy Programmes were genuinely intergenerational – they provided quality teaching for parents on their own, for children on their own, and for parents and children together.*

9.16 Summary

The outline story is that:

- the Basic Skills Agency had a very clear purpose, expressed in a very precise set of guidelines

- the Programmes were very carefully picked

- so were the teachers

- the '12 weeks x 8 hours = 96 hours' model focused everyone's minds on achieving a great deal in a fixed time

- joint staffing and fixed time ensured detailed joint planning

- the parents were volunteers, and came to the Programmes with strong aspirations and motivation

- the Wordpower accreditation requirement gave parents a clear picture of what they could achieve for themselves, and the recruitment details gave them a clear picture of what they could achieve for their children

- the clear objectives for themselves and their children, and knowledge of the amount of time available, gave parents joint purpose which encouraged group cohesion

- because of the quality of the teachers and their joint planning, the teaching was excellent, for parents and children and both together

- the clear and open planning, excellent teaching and group cohesion in parents' sessions laid half of the basis for the joint sessions

- in particular, the courses gave a massive boost to the parents' confidence

- meanwhile, the clear planning and excellent teaching in children's sessions laid the other half of the basis for the joint sessions

- so in the joint sessions everything dovetailed, and they provided parents with immediate feedback on what they could achieve with their children

- the Programmes were more carefully structured, and therefore more effective, than comparable initiatives in the United States.

RESULT: SUCCESS

CHAPTER TEN

Why were the Programmes successful?
(2) Material factors

The human, process factors in the Programmes' success were dealt with in the previous chapter. This chapter deals with the material preconditions or prerequisites for success.

10.1 Finances: unit cost and value for money

The majority (75 per cent) of the financing of the Programmes was provided, through the Agency, by the Department for Education and Employment and the Welsh Office, and the other 25 per cent by a range of local providers. The local lead partners were a Local Education Authority, a County Council, a Metropolitan Borough, and a Community College.

With the finance provided, the Programmes were highly effective in boosting the parents' and children's literacy and the parents' ability to help their children. But did they provide good value for money? The rest of this section provides a calculation of a unit cost, and makes a judgement on value for money.

10.1.1 Cost per participant-learning hour

This calculation is based on the costs of courses which the Programmes mounted in addition to those originally contracted, but still on the full Agency model and with the same balance of funding from the Agency and local partners (75/25 per cent). These courses were the fairest basis on which to calculate a unit cost because they did not have to bear any of the development costs of the courses for which the Programmes' original funding was provided, though they were just as much part of the NFER evaluation as the originally contracted courses.

These 'extra' courses cost, on average, £8,000. The typical number of participants was nine parents, plus 10 participating children, plus five children in the crèche: a total of 24. Dividing £8,000 first by 24 (for the participants) and then by the 96 hours yielded

a cost per 'participant-learning hour' of £3.47.

Since attendance rates were so high, it seemed unnecessary to adjust this calculation (upwards) to allow for absences.

10.1.2 Judgement on value for money

In basing a judgment on this unit cost, the evaluators bore in mind that:

- *the Programmes had produced very strong quantifiable benefits for the participants*

- *both parents and children had benefited greatly; therefore every pound spent had done 'double duty'*

- *some of the most powerful effects for the parents (motivation, confidence, commitment to lifetime learning, better relationships and communication with their children) were unquantifiable*

- *some of the benefits for children may well show up only in the longer term*

- *some of the benefits for society of this investment in education now may also show up only in the longer term, through heading off troubles (such as educational and possibly therefore social failure, including imprisonment) before they occur (St. Pierre et al., 1994, presented US evidence that this is so).*

On this basis and for the benefits to both parents and children, the evaluators judged that **the Family Literacy Programmes represented good value for money.**

10.2 Premises

All initiatives need a base, and all four Programmes were promised by their local providers a main site which would as far as possible meet all their requirements in one place. This promise was delivered in full or nearly so for three of the Programmes before they began teaching.

At the one main site where everything was in one place, this encompassed, within an area perhaps 15 metres x 20 metres, an office, a parents' room, an Early Years room, a room for the crèche, a kitchen, two toilets and a securely fenced outdoor play area. At two other Programmes' main sites these elements were all present, not contiguously but within a few metres.

The fourth Programme, however, was bedevilled for its first two terms by its main premises not being ready. Staff there operated in corridors, in corners of classrooms where primary classes were also operating, and in the staff room and hall. Integrated premises were eventually provided. The staff here felt severely hampered by the inadequate premises in which they began teaching.

All the Programmes ran courses for varying numbers of terms at several sites besides their main one. Except for an office, in principle these required the same facilities as the main site, but in practice premises varied considerably. At one extreme, imaginative use was made of an existing Young Women's Project where Early Years and crèche were in separated parts of one room, while parents' sessions were held in a study room across the yard which was the play area. At the other extreme, another Programme in a particular term ran courses at two temporary sites. In one, sessions were held in a corridor. There was a fair amount of room but it was easy to get distracted and there could be quite a lot of noise. The Programme staff had to try and time their breaks to coincide with the noisy times. At the other temporary site, there was a room set aside for the parents but it was in 'a terrible state'. Apart from needing redecorating, it was dirty and generally unpleasant. This was the only room available in the school and, as there were so many parents wanting to do the course, they felt they had to put up with it.

Whatever the premises, Programme staff used them as best they could, and this provision represented a part of the contribution from local partners.

10.3 Proximity to participants' homes

The great majority of participating **families lived within feasible walking distance** of the site they attended. Some, however, lived at greater distances, and it was part of the Agency's requirements that this should not prevent them participating. Where the numbers involved were small, Programme staff gave lifts. A few parents travelled to and from courses by bus, and received expenses for this. In two Programmes for one term each, groups of parents who were keen to attend but who lived on the far side of the town and had no easy public transport for the journey were brought to and from the course by taxi. For such families, participation would otherwise have been impossible. However, these arrangements, though manageable, were awkward, and were not repeated. Several coordinators said they would always try to put a course on where the families were, and it seems clear that proximity of courses to target families was more manageable than arranging transport.

10.4 Crèche provision

The Agency insisted that all sites of all Programmes should have crèche provision for any children the participating parents might have who were under three years of age at the start of the course, and that the crèche should be open at all times when the Programme was operating.

The crèches were not formally covered by the evaluation remit, but informal observation suggested that the provision was of high quality because of the skill and experience of the relevant staff; and that the crèches were in fact often open when the

Programmes were not strictly speaking operating - for instance, at 'taster' sessions and during coffee mornings for previous students.

The Programme Coordinators and parents who were interviewed were emphatic that the **crèche provision was essential for many parents**. Very few or none of those who had a child or children under three would have been able to attend otherwise. And the restriction on under-threes being present in parents' or joint sessions seemed entirely justified. Among the 35 relevant sessions observed, there was only one (a parents' session) when a crèche child was with the parent: the child was grizzling and a disruptive presence.

10.5 Appropriate staffing levels

Staffing was at an appropriate level. That level was partly determined by the Agency's Quality Standards for Adult Basic Skills courses, and partly by legal considerations. Parents' sessions could be run by one teacher, but all children's (and therefore joint) sessions required both an Early Years teacher and an assistant (usually a nursery nurse). Also, social services regulations dictated the number of crèche workers required to be present, and set a limit on crèche places according to the space available. This in turn occasionally limited the number of parents able to attend.

The largest parents' group reported was 13, and the smallest four, while the average, and most typical number, was nine.

Children's groups also varied, from 14 to four. With appropriate division for group work, this meant that in some children's sessions the child/teacher ratio was as low as 2:1 (and one such session was observed), and was never higher than 7:1.

10.6 Good materials

Materials were of good quality and in general sufficient. There were ample resources for parents (dictionaries, information leaflets, etc.), and each Programme had at least one computer, at its main site. Adult Basic Skills teachers devised a great many stimulus sheets – as many as 15 in one session observed. So frequent were such materials that one Adult Basic Skills Coordinator was heard by a fieldworker to say 'Here's my first sheet of the day', and this quip was received with familiar amusement by the parents present.

When permanent premises were in use, both parents' rooms and especially children's rooms (both Early Years and crèche) were attractively furnished and decorated. Before teaching began some Programme staff put their own time into painting and decorating their main premises, and displays and (where possible) room arrangements were regularly varied. Books and toys were excellent.

The only problem noted here by Programme staff was that only one example of some items of equipment for Early Years sessions was available. This meant that activities requiring such equipment could not be offered simultaneously at more than one site.

Often, effective planning avoided problems, but even the best planning could not prevent the occasional disappointment when a spontaneously arising activity could not happen because the item required was unavoidably detained elsewhere.

10.7 Collaborative local partners and schools

The financial support given by local partners has already been mentioned. Because the Programmes crossed phases of the education system and therefore sectors and 'territories', close collaboration was essential. Line management was provided by senior Adult Basic Skills organisers; in each case the support given by these managers was unstinting. It often involved keeping the initiative before the eyes of those who had local financial control and/or who could endorse the initiative's achievements. This will be crucial to the Programmes' future.

In some cases, local newspapers produced recruitment leaflets, and local library services provided support such as book collections and story-tellers. Often, appropriate LEA Advisers and social services representatives were on the local Steering Committee, and they gave advice freely to the Programme staff.

Also important to the Programmes' effectiveness were the institutions on or alongside whose premises they operated. At most sites (including all the main ones) these were primary schools, though one Young Women's Project has already been mentioned. Programme Coordinators were unanimous in saying that good relations with 'host' schools had been important to them.

The importance of good relations was highlighted in the one case where they started off poor. At a new site in one Programme, communications before the course started had not been clear, and for a whole term the headteacher and class teachers communicated with Programme staff only through a support teacher.

However, the Adult Basic Skills Coordinator felt that, after the 12 weeks, the school staff had been able to see that the course was non-threatening and was not trying to take credit for the school's work: 'We were actually complementing what they were doing'. She thought that there was now a feeling of camaraderie; school staff would ask for copies of resources and would lend copies of theirs.

Two schools which hosted Programmes' main sites provided stories of great support. At one, the Programme's parents' room was a classroom in the school's main building. A terrapin classroom burnt down, and extra pressure on space in the school was caused. The headteacher nevertheless did not take the parents' room back. The other school housed the main site of the Programme whose promised premises were not provided at the opening of the Programme. Here, the headteacher arranged that the school hall should not be used by the school for a term on the days the Programme operated, in order to make it available to the Programme. Both incidents imply not only support for the initiative, but also that the headteachers believed that the Programme children were benefiting so much that the 'investment' was worthwhile.

The general picture of relations with schools was therefore good. However, there was one issue which proved a constant source of tension, namely the Programmes' requirement that qualifying children who were in school should be withdrawn from school to attend Family Literacy sessions. This issue is discussed in section 11.3.

Two strategic aspects of the relationship with host institutions deserve mention. First, the coordinators felt that where a course was based in a school, it tended to attract mostly parents from that school's catchment area – parents from other schools' catchments seemed to have to cross a 'territorial' boundary to participate and were less likely to do so. The course in the Young Women's Project seemed to prove this in reverse; parents from several schools' catchments seemed equally happy to come, just because it was not sited in anyone's 'own' school.

Secondly, it seemed crucial to the success of many courses that they were based in primary schools, and not in, for example, further education establishments (as Adult Basic Skills courses tend to be), even where one of the local partners or the local lead body was an FE college. The coordinators felt that the psychological barrier to enrolment for many parents would have been insurmountable in an FE building.

Such locations would also have posed geographical problems for many parents. As most of the courses were on primary school sites, the large number of participating parents who had other children could deliver those children already at the school to school, and any younger children to the crèche (if not under the same roof as the course), and then themselves to the course, all within a few minutes. Any greater distance would have deterred many parents.

10.8 Effective recruitment

For the sorts of reasons just implied, recruitment of parents needed to be very local to be effective. Also, it had to attract volunteers, since students were not to come through referral (for instance, from the social services). And one of the Programmes was based in an area where it was known that (ordinary) adult literacy courses are poorly supported. Also, the emphasis of the recruitment publicity had to be sensitive to parents' feelings about their own literacy (see page 31).

In interviews early in the evaluation, the coordinators described a range of strategies they had employed: publicity in local newspapers and radio programmes, leaflets of various types, preliminary ('taster') sessions and/or coffee mornings, personal approaches by teachers or the coordinators themselves at host schools. The coordinators felt that the media and leaflet methods had brought in very few parents, and that the other, more direct, approaches had brought in virtually all of them, especially in the early stages. This was largely borne out by the parent interview findings shown in Table 10.1.

Table 10.1: **How parents found out about the course**

Cohort	Summer 1994	Autumn 1994	Spring 1995	Summer 1995	Total
Number of respondents	32	39	35	17	123
Number of references					
Letter	11	6	18	7	42
Through school (unspecified)	9	6	15	6	36
Poster	6	11	6	6	29
Course tutor	8	9	5	0	22
Meeting	5	5	6	6	22
Word of mouth	4	5	12	0	21
Class teacher	2	14	1	1	18
Taster course	0	4	6	6	16
Friend	5	4	1	0	10
Coffee Morning	0	4	0	1	5
Previous course	0	5	3	0	8

The proportion of posters and letters (taken together) remained constant. Though the numbers of references to recruitment by a 'Course tutor' seemed to fall, it was, presumably, tutors who were involved in arranging taster courses and meetings which, proportionately, grew. Though not frequently referred to, where used, very locally, the coffee morning approach was effective – especially for accurate targeting. If any of the respondents had been targeted for the course, none seemed to realise it.

There was a reference in one area to 40 parents attending a taster evening. On tasters, generally, where they were used, they were appreciated – at least by the parents who went on to take the course. They seemed to help with 'confidence' (as did 'going with a friend'). Courage was also required to start the course, and support was needed, especially in the early stages, to sustain that courage:

> *I was put in the Wednesday group at first but found I didn't know anyone. It was also rather a large group, so I asked if I could swop to the Thursday group. This was a much smaller group and I knew the other parents, so it was much better for me.*

Direct, local approaches had therefore given many parents the initial courage they needed.

What is also noticeable about Table 10.1 is the complete absence of references to media publicity. After the Summer term of 1994, the Programmes abandoned such methods. They continued producing leaflets, but made them part of their direct approaches, as items to be handed direct to potential students, rather than leaving them in 'likely' places to be picked up. In one Programme, in one term group at a non-central site, only two parents had been recruited through leaflets unsupported by any more direct approach. Almost all of this group had attended a one-off First Aid day at the end of the previous term and been recruited through that.

As the evaluation proceeded, students from previous courses became effective recruiters for later ones, where a centre was used in successive terms (which meant principally at the main sites). The outcome of the recruitment strategies, in terms of the characteristics of the parents who attended courses, was discussed in Chapter 5.

One or two of the coordinators, when interviewed, raised the issue of the possible impact on recruitment of parents (usually) having to commit themselves to a whole school day. They feared this might have deterred some potential students. However, several other coordinators stressed that many parents wanted the 1.5-day pattern, and had not been put off by it. Where adjustments to that pattern occurred, they were entirely due either to the days and part days of the week when premises were available, or to the need to assuage schools' concerns about withdrawal (see section 11.3), or both.

In their interviews, coordinators were also asked about the emphasis, within recruitment approaches, on the possible benefit to parents' own literacy. They had been very sensitive to the possibility of alienating parents by any hint that their skills were deficient; because of this, their early publicity mentioned only the benefits for children. As time went on, they became more open with parents about the possible benefits for them, while still realising that this issue had to be handled with tact.

10.9 Time

This subsection considers not only the obvious topic of time on task, but also elapsed time.

10.9.1 Elapsed time

Typically, the period between the first and last sessions of a course was 11 weeks and one day. In the case of the children's vocabulary and early reading development, it has already been shown that the lapse of time during the course was **not** a sufficient explanation for their gains; the children made significantly more progress than would have been expected simply from 'normal' growth and development.

Given this, it is also very improbable that the growth observed in children's early writing development during the courses would have been so pronounced if they had not been involved in the courses, and had therefore made 'normal' progress.

A high proportion of the parents fell into an age-range (20-39) at which it has been shown (see Appendix, section A.4.3) that they might have been expected to make some very small amount of progress during the courses. But the amounts of progress made during the courses were, on average, far from tiny, and nothing else was going on in these parents' lives that might have accounted for this. The evaluators concluded that the parents' improvements too were the direct result of the Programmes, and that elapsed time was not a plausible explanation of those improvements.

10.9.2 Time on task

On the other hand, time on task probably was part of the explanation of both the parents' and the children's gains. It routinely emerges as a significant factor in educational interventions, and there was no reason to suppose that this initiative was different in this respect. The participants received up to 96 hours of tuition during the course sessions, and there was ample evidence of the work that parents put in in their own time both on their own skills and on helping their children. Though this factor is indispensable and may seem obvious, it deserved to be made explicit.

10.10 Summary

With the exception of elapsed time, all the factors considered in this chapter were judged to have played a part in the Programmes' success, namely good premises, proximity to participants' homes, crèche provision, appropriate staffing levels, good materials, and adequate finance to provide all this, plus collaborative local partners, effective recruitment, and time on task.

The cost per 'participant-learning hour' was estimated as £3.47.

In the evaluators' judgement, **the Family Literacy Programmes represented good value for money.**

CHAPTER ELEVEN

Possible barriers to success

___

11.1 Unrealistic aspirations by a few parents for their children

There were hints that a few parents' aspirations for their children were considered unrealistic by the coordinators. One gave the example of a child who had not had any nursery education at all, and whose skills were very poor. The child also had some special learning needs, and the parent joined the course specifically to help him overcome them. The coordinator felt that by the end of the course the parent realised that the child was always going to have those problems but now she would be able to help him work with them:

> *Parents may start by thinking they want their child to be top of the class, but eventually they realise that that is not always the best thing for the child. They come to understand that the child should enjoy what they are doing and get the most out of it that they can. Some parents think that their child has really bad behaviour problems, but they realise that their child is perfectly normal. It may be that they're expecting too much age-wise from that child.*

Another coordinator also said that some parents' aspirations for their children became more realistic during the course:

> *for example they (no longer) have an idealised notion of what six-year-olds should be able to do, they lose the insecurity of competitive comparing with other people's children, they're more tuned to their child being happy and rewarded from school.*

A moment when two parents had such an insight was observed. A primary headteacher had been visiting a parents' session to talk about developing children's early writing skills . When she left, the adult tutor went out of the room with her for a minute. Before she returned, two of the parents commented:

> *(I've) been doing it all wrong.*
>
> *She (her child) is listening but you don't think she is.*

These remarks seemed to imply, respectively, that these parents had been trying too didactic an approach for a young child, and expecting constant feedback from a child to demonstrate attention, when that child was absorbing a great deal nonetheless.

This is not meant to suggest that many parents had unrealistic expectations, still less that the courses blunted realistic aspirations. Far from it; the evaluators concluded that, where aspirations had been tempered, they had been tempered from too high to be realistic to strong and realistic.

11.2 Variation in effectiveness of visiting speakers

From the parent interviews it was clear that most visitors were effective, but also that a few were not. A particularly effective session (despite being held in awkward premises) was on science. The visitor was fairly directive but had brought along several very good activities, and gave very good advice to parents on using them with children. One activity tied in very closely with the section of the Key Stage 1 curriculum on floating and sinking.

One of the few ineffective visitors (observed in a joint session) not only talked at a level well beyond the children's understanding, but also did not bring any of the promised activities and therefore made the session much shorter than the staff had been led to believe. Fortunately, on this occasion they had been forewarned by a colleague who had had the same experience with the same visitor on a different site the day before, and they had had time (which the colleague had not) to bring along activities intended for the following week.

Such problems can occur in any project. What was also clear from the parent interviews was that such complaints were confined to the earlier terms and that Programme staff soon learned to avoid some visitors, and to give those they did invite clear preparation on time, the level at which to pitch explanations for children, and so on. Some parents interviewed in the Summer term 1995 reported successful sessions from visiting speakers criticised by those in earlier terms.

11.3 Withdrawal of children from school classes

The Agency's model of Family Literacy declared as eligible for the initiative any parent who had at least one child aged between 3:00 and 6:11 at the start of the course. This meant that some participating children were already attending nursery or primary school; and those already in primary school might be in Reception or in Year 1 or Year 2. The model further stipulated that parents could not attend without bringing their 'qualifying' children with them, so that some participating children were being withdrawn from school for 1.5 days a week.

106

The Agency's rationale for overlapping the initiative's age-range with the infant school was to avoid giving the impression that Family Literacy was relevant only to pre-schoolers, and to reinforce its links with the Early Years curriculum.

As a coordinator put it:

> *This is vital for creating a **family** and not a classroom approach and atmosphere because of the mix of ages. Also, if we had targeted single year-groups, this would have evoked even more anxious comparisons from parents.*

The 3-6 age-range element caused varying reactions in the schools from which children were being withdrawn. Some schools appeared to welcome the extra provision for pupils who would figure in their list of those 'at risk of educational failure', while other schools objected to any loss of school time. The tension was at its highest in one Programme in the summer term 1994 over a number of Year 2 pupils, who were being given the national curriculum Key Stage 1 Standard Assessment Tasks that term; the schools concerned seemed to feel that any absence from the school classroom disrupted the children's education and might lower their KS1 attainments. This tension was not entirely absent from any of the Programmes.

Several strategies were employed to reduce or avoid the problem. In the Programme where the tension was highest, for that term some children's sessions operated not on 1.5 school days, but on the basis of alternate Saturday mornings and some after-school sessions. The following term there were some lunch-time sessions, and Year 2 children were withdrawn only in the afternoons. In another Programme, the Early Years Coordinator decided in the Autumn term 1994 not to withdraw any nursery or reception children, but to work with them in their school classrooms. This was because these children were all very new in school. The coordinator also put a student nursery nurse into the reception class, and withdrew only the Year 1 children already established in school. The following term this pattern was modified somewhat. Nursery children were supported in their classroom for two sessions and withdrawn for one – this was what the teachers at the school preferred.

In another Programme too, in the Autumn term 1994 some children were new both to the Programme and to nursery school. Some of these children therefore attended the Programme for only half the sessions. The Early Years Coordinator felt that the school might ask that in 1995 no children should start school and the Programme simultaneously, but should have their entry to the Programme delayed by a term. During one joint session at this Programme the fieldworker observed children being taken out of the session and back to class by their regular teachers.

In all the Programmes, there was a conscious decision, apparently implemented early in the 1994/95 school year, to re-define the target age-range as 'age 3 up to 6-year-olds in Year 1', and therefore to avoid recruiting children who were already in Year 2; this reduced the proportion of pupils aged 6:00-6:11 at the start of a course. This decision was apparently taken in consultation with the host schools and the Agency, and resulted in the removal of the tension over the issue.

In the evaluators' judgement, the decision was a justified modification of the Agency's model, since it removed most of the source of tension, without abandoning the principle of overlapping Family Literacy with the early school years.

11.4 Intermittent sites

Most courses on most sites were highly effective. That said, there were factors which did slightly limit the effectiveness of some courses in reaching those in most need. It was shown in Chapter 5 that relatively few parents were recruited whose skills were initially below Level 1 of the Agency's Communication Standards. Such parents accounted for 18 per cent of those recruited; the Agency had set a target of at least 30 per cent.

It was also shown in Chapter 5 that:

- *the shortfall may have been because there were fewer such parents in the courses' catchment areas than had been thought, and that*

- *some success was achieved in recruiting greater numbers of such parents over time, particularly at continuing sites.*

It has also been suggested that the psychological limit to the catchment area for many parents is that of their children's school; and that a successful way to attract parents from more than one school is to mount courses on a 'neutral' site. However, it also seems clear that some neutral sites would be unsuitable, particularly further education buildings.

The implication of all this is that, if parents at or below Foundation Level are to be recruited in greater numbers, courses may have to be mounted for a number of terms consecutively at a suitable neutral site in order to achieve this, and not for only a term or two, or intermittently, at any site. Even then, it may be unrealistic to expect that the numbers of parents at or below Foundation Level would ever be very large in any one area; therefore it may be that the supply of such parents even to a site which was very successful in recruiting them might not last long. The further implication may therefore be that there would be a limit to the number of terms for which it would be effective to mount courses consecutively even at such sites. How many terms that might be could be established only by very careful monitoring of recruitment patterns. But it may be that the most effective pattern of all may require neither permanent nor intermittent sites, but a rolling programme of changing sites with stability at each site for a number of terms.

11.5 Other barriers to success

Very few members of ethnic and linguistic minorities were recruited onto the four continuing Demonstration Programmes. In disseminating the model to areas where there are many potential recruits from these minorities sensitive adaptation will be needed.

Attempts to provide parents with transport to attend courses proved largely unmanageable, and courses needed to be close to target families' homes to be effective. This reinforces the need for courses to change their sites on a rolling basis.

CHAPTER TWELVE

Lessons and recommendations

―――――――

12.1 Starting points

- The parents who were recruited onto these Programmes were validly targeted: they were **poorly qualified**, lived in areas of **multiple deprivation**, and had **low levels of literacy**. The Programmes' recruitment policy had therefore been successful.

- The parents brought to the Programmes **strong motivation on their children's** behalf.

- Most of their children were severely disadvantaged for learning by low scores in language and literacy, at great risk of educational failure, and in urgent need of help.

12.2 Benefits to the children

- The children made **greater-than-expected average improvements in vocabulary during the courses and in the 12 weeks after them**, and normal progress in the next six months.

- Exactly the same was true of the children's progress in reading.

- In writing, they made substantial average improvements during the courses, and in the 12 weeks after them, and in the next six months.

- Thus many children had benefited in **all three aspects of language.**

- Some of the specific **gains made by the children were:**
  - the standardised mean score for **vocabulary rose from 85 to 93**
  - the proportion whose lack of vocabulary would leave them **struggling in school** fell from 54 per cent to 31 per cent
  - the proportion whose vocabulary would leave them **severely disadvantaged for learning** fell from 17 per cent to six per cent
  - the standardised mean score for **reading rose from 84 to 92**
  - the proportion whose low reading level would leave them **struggling in school** fell from 67 per cent to 35 per cent

- the proportion whose reading level would leave them **severely disadvantaged** for learning fell from 24 per cent to nine per cent
- during the courses, the proportion of school-age **children who had not yet made** the crucial transition to writing words fell from 62 per cent to 43 per cent.

- Therefore the initiative **was working for the great majority of children; a high proportion of them were better equipped for school learning.**

- But a minority had not made such good progress, and would need further specialised help.

- **All parents observed an improvement in their children's spoken language.**

- Many parents also observed **improvements in their children's literacy,** and in their **attitudes to learning and confidence.**

12.3 Boost to the parents' ability to help their children

- There were **substantial increases in literacy-related home activities,** and these became **firmly embedded** in family practice.

- Parents also reported **substantial increases in their ability to help their children** with language and literacy and in their **confidence** in doing so.

- Many parents also reported that their **relationship with their child had greatly improved.**

- Parents seemed to feel that **a barrier between school practice and home activities had been crossed.**

- Parents were beginning to **enjoy their own success as they saw their children's** progress.

12.4 Benefits to parents

- During the courses, **the parents improved their average reading test scores by five per cent** of the maximum score.

- During the courses, **the parents improved their average writing score by 10 per cent** of the starting level.

- **Both improvements were sustained** afterwards.

- **95 per cent of all the parents attained partial or full accreditation of a level of Wordpower.**

- Over half (52 per cent) of the parents responding also referred to **a growth in their confidence,** and many reported other improvements in social skills.

- The number of parents actively involved in their children's schools increased significantly.

- At the end of the course, **over 80 per cent of parents planned to go on studying, and 12 weeks after the courses 70 per cent were actually doing a further course**.

12.5 The fulfilling of the Agency's aims, requirements and objectives

- The Agency's triple aims were to boost parents' literacy, parents' ability to help their children, and children's literacy; **all three were fulfilled**.

- Of the requirements on the Programmes set by the Agency (see section 2.2), all but two were met in full. The exceptions were:
  - the main site premises for one Programme were not ready until about two terms into the initiative
  - the Agency's target for the proportion of parents at or below Foundation Level was 30 per cent; the achieved sample was 18 per cent – but this target was probably unrealistic (see section 5.3.3).

- The requirement on parents was that each had to have at least one child aged between 3 years 0 months and 6 years 11 months at the beginning of the course, and both parent and child had to attend.
  - The first part of this was met in full.
  - Attendance by children had in some cases to be modified so that they attended some sessions at the Programme and received the rest of their Family Literacy support in their classroom. This was done because of host schools' worries over withdrawing children from classes (see section 11.3). The problem was solved by adjusting the age-range for qualifying children to 'aged from 3 years 0 months up to 6-year-olds in Year 1', and by convincing host schools that the children were benefiting more by spending some time at Family Literacy than by remaining in the classroom full-time.

The objectives in terms of outcomes set by the Agency for the Programmes (see section 2.2) included those listed below. For each objective the extent to which it was met is noted.

- Involvement, over the first five terms of teaching, of approximately 150 parents and 180 children:
  - all four Programmes met this target.

- A retention rate of 75 per cent of families for the 12-week period of the courses:
  - **the achieved retention rate was 91 per cent** and attendance rates were consistently high

112

- Improvement in the literacy of 80 per cent of parents:
  - during the courses, on average **the parents improved their reading score by 5 per cent of the maximum score, and their writing score by 10 per cent from the starting level.**

- Achievement of accreditation by 70 per cent of parents:
  - **the achieved accreditation rate was close to 100 per cent.**

- Improved knowledge of methods of fostering emergent literacy by 80 per cent of parents:
  - **all parents who completed the course gained greater understanding** of how to help their children with reading and writing.

- Improvement in the emergent literacy skills of 80 per cent of children:
  - as a group, the children made **greater-than-expected gains not only in reading and writing, but also in vocabulary.**

Overall, the Agency's aims, requirements and objectives were fulfilled in great detail.

12.6 The realisation of parents' aspirations for themselves and their children

The parents' aspirations for themselves and their children were described in section 5.2. The principal aspirations are re-stated below, each followed by a note of the extent to which it was realised.

- The predominant hope that parents expressed (90 per cent or more in both writing and interviews) was to learn how to help their children to learn to read and write:
  - **every item on the Home Activities questionnaire showed a significant increase during the course**
  - of the parents interviewed at the end of the courses and at 12-week follow-up, **almost all agreed that they had learnt how to help their children**
  - in writing too, **every parent mentioned at least one aspect of increased knowledge.**

- Fifty-eight per cent of parents wanted to improve their own basic skills:
  - **the parents improved their average reading score by 5 per cent, and their average writing score by 10 per cent.**

- Among the less frequently mentioned of parents' aspirations for themselves were gaining patience, confidence and a qualification:
  - all of these were met for many more parents than initially mentioned them.

113

- Almost all parents also achieved accreditation of another skill developed during the course.

- The parents' hope that **their children would benefit** had to be inferred, mainly from their desire to learn to help them and from the fact that **over 90 per cent of the parents had never attended a basic skills course before:**
  - as a group, **the children made substantial gains.**
  - the parents expressed **great satisfaction with their children's progress.**

12.7 Bonus effects

Not only were all the Agency's aims fulfilled and the parents' hopes realised, but the Programmes' achievements also extended **considerably beyond the stated targets:**

- the Programmes had acted as **women's access courses**

- all the gains made by parents and children during the course were **at least sustained** up to 9 months afterwards, and in many cases there were **further improvements**

- **communication** between parents and children **improved markedly**

- so did their mutual enjoyment of literacy and related activities

- parents reported considerable improvement in their ability to **communicate with their children's teachers**

- through the extra courses set up during the lifetime of the evaluation, the Agency's **model was shown to be applicable** in different settings.

12.8 Factors in the Programmes' success

- The following factors were all judged to have been effective as material prerequisites to the Programmes' success (see chapter 10):
  - good premises, proximity to participants' homes, crèche provision, appropriate staffing ratios, well-designed and attractive materials and resources, the finances to support all this, collaborative local partners and schools, direct local recruitment (including recruitment by 'graduates' of the courses), and parents' and children's time on task.

- The cost per 'participant-learning hour' was estimated as £3.47.

- In the evaluators' judgement, **the Family Literacy Programmes represented good value for money.**

114

More important in the process of creating the Programmes' success were the human factors (see chapter 9):

- the clear **purpose** set by the Agency, avoiding grandiose aims but extending from reading to the whole of language development
- the careful **selection** of Programmes and teachers
- the **focusing** of everyone's minds on achieving a great deal in a fixed time
- detailed and collaborative **joint planning**
- the strong aspirations and motivation that **parents brought** to the Programmes, and their volunteer status
- the clear **pictures** given to parents of **what they could achieve** for themselves (by the Wordpower accreditation requirement), and for their children (by the recruitment details)
- the joint purpose and **group cohesion** achieved by parents
- the **excellent and reflective teaching** given to both parents and children
- the massive boost given to the parents' **confidence**
- the genuinely intergenerational nature of the courses
- the **creative synthesis in the joint sessions**, with their immediate **feedback**, the sense of **achievement** they gave parents, and the **enjoyment and learning** they gave children.

Comparisons with intergenerational family literacy programmes which have been evaluated in the United States, and which have in general been found to be less effective, suggest that the **following differences were crucial:**

- *the Family Literacy Programmes avoided grandiose social and socioeconomic aims*

- *the Family Literacy Programmes avoided over-concentration on reading, and genuinely focused also on talking and writing*

- *in the Family Literacy Programmes, all participating parents were volunteers*

- *in the Family Literacy Programmes, the fixed time limit concentrated all minds*

- *the Family Literacy Programmes were genuinely intergenerational: they provided quality teaching for parents on their own, for children on their own, and for parents and children together.*

115

12.9 Possible barriers to success

The hindrances to success were few (see chapter 11), and some were resolved during the initiative.

- Some parents might come with expectations for their children that are so high that they are unrealisable. Where this occurred, Programme staff tackled the matter sensitively – parents modified the expectations to become realistic even if still strong.

- A few visiting speakers were not particularly effective.

- The withdrawal issue has been discussed in sections 11.3 and 12.5.

- The difficulty of recruiting parents at or below Foundation Level was not fully overcome, but possible strategies to maximise the chances of recruiting them began to emerge (section 11.4).

- Very few members of ethnic and linguistic minorities were recruited, but the model should be applicable in areas where they would be strongly represented.

- Attempts to enable parents to attend courses at more than walking distance or an easy bus ride from home proved difficult to manage. This may restrict the catchment area of many centres, and reinforces the case for not staying at any centre indefinitely.

- Some of the children with the lowest initial scores and therefore in greatest need did not return for testing at the end of the courses. Also, a few children made little progress, and fell relatively further behind. For some children, therefore, further provision would be needed.

- The cost per participant-learning hour (see section 10.1.1) might be seen as an obstacle, but this was not the evaluators' judgment (see above, section 12.8), and needs to be set against the presumed social cost of doing nothing.

12.10 Recommendations

- Family Literacy alone cannot solve all literacy problems, but as a complement to other initiatives and as part of a mixed and targeted set of strategies it **can contribute powerfully to the improvement of literacy, and should be enabled to do so.**

- The **clear purpose** and **fixed time** of the Programmes were crucial to their success, and should be maintained.

- The **voluntary nature** of the Programmes should be maintained.

- The Programmes must also remain **fully intergenerational**.

116

- More effective methods of recruiting parents with severe literacy problems should be sought and tried out.

- The initiative needs to reach out to members of ethnic and linguistic minorities.

- In connection with both points, the policy of careful geographical placement of courses needs to be maintained. More 'neutral' sites, those not on primary school premises, might be advantageous in areas of strong loyalty to local schools. The most effective pattern might be neither permanent nor intermittent sites, but a **rolling programme of changing sites** with stability at each site for a number of terms.

- Having all elements of a course **under one roof** was undoubtedly the best arrangement, and should be adopted wherever possible. If one element (for example the crèche) has to be in a separate building, the distance should be no more than a few hundred metres.

- Both crèche provision and joint Adult Basic Skills/Early Years staffing remain crucial to the identity and focus of the initiative, and dilution of these principles should be avoided.

- The structure of separate and joint sessions also needs to be retained, because of the benefit parents derive from immediate, supervised practice with their children.

- The practice of timetabling the parents' and children's sessions in parallel is not strictly logically necessary, and one Programme found it possible for a while to run them at different times, and the Early Years Coordinator made strategic use of the opportunity to visit parents' sessions. However, the parallel arrangement seems the most manageable, since otherwise some parents might require crèche facilities for younger children for more than three sessions a week. Any other arrangement might also make it more difficult for Adult Basic Skills and Early Years staff to collaborate as fully as is needed.

- The slightly revised age-range for children (from 3:00 up to 6-year-olds in Year 1, avoiding children already in Year 2) should be maintained. However, further narrowing of the age-range should be avoided, because the overlap with the school years reinforces the **family** nature of the provision, and helps to bring schools in as partners and to convince them of the value of the courses.

- If Further Education colleges wish to provide Family Literacy courses, they may have to circumvent the possible psychological barrier for some parents of attending classes on a Further Education site. To do so, colleges would need to work in close partnership with Local Education Authorities.

- Effective collaboration between local partners is essential to the success of such programmes on the ground, especially where all funding has to be raised locally. This is the **ownership** aspect of successful educational innovation.

- But also crucial for successful educational innovation is **endorsement**, the feeling on the part of providers that they have the visible and practical backing of influential bodies and individuals. For the continued success of the Family Literacy initiative, such backing needs to come from central government. Moreover, given the scale of need (see the opening sentence of chapter 1), this backing needs to be not only moral but also and crucially financial.

An LEA officer with responsibility for one of the Programmes was heard to say that initiatives come and go, and some seem to have relatively little impact. This one, he thought, was the most effective he had seen in 30 years. Similarly, the executive summary of the evaluation team's interim report to the Agency was said by one journalist (MacLeod, 1995) to contain an 'extraordinarily enthusiastic verdict from the normally tight-lipped researchers of the National Foundation for Educational Research'. The evaluators would wish to comment that they do not 'loosen their lip' unless they are convinced by the evidence.

- *The Basic Skills Agency's Family Literacy Demonstration Programmes initiative has achieved great success.*

- *The members of the team evaluating it judged it to be one of the most effective initiatives they had ever encountered, and well worth building on.*

- *Our principal recommendation is therefore that the Family Literacy initiative should be continued and made available more widely across the country.*

References

THE BASIC SKILLS AGENCY (1993). *Parents and their Children: the intergenerational effect of poor basic skills*. London: Adult Literacy and Basic Skills Unit.

THE BASIC SKILLS AGENCY (1995). *Older and Younger: the basic skills of different age groups*. London: Adult Literacy and Basic Skills Unit.

BARTON, D. (1995). 'Exploring family literacy.' *Reading*, **29**, 3, 2-4.

BROOKS, G., FOXMAN, D. and GORMAN, T.P. (1995). *Standards in Literacy and Numeracy: 1948-1994*. (National Commission on Education Briefing new series no.7) London: National Commission on Education.

BYNNER, J. and STEEDMAN, J. (1995). *Difficulties with Basic Skills: findings from the 1970 British Cohort Study*. London: Basic Skills Agency.

DICKINSON, D.K. (1994). 'Epilogue: what next?' In D.K. Dickinson (ed.) *Bridges to Literacy: children, families, and schools*. Cambridge, MA and Oxford: Blackwell, 285-9.

EKINSMYTH, C. AND BYNNER, J. (1994). *The Basic Skills of Young Adults*. London: Adult Literacy and Basic Skills Unit.

GORMAN, T.P. (1981). 'A survey of attainment and progress of learners in adult literacy schemes.' *Educational Research*, **23**, 3, 190-8.

GORMAN, T.P. AND BROOKS, G. (1996). *Assessing Young Children's Writing: a step by step guide*. London: Basic Skills Agency.

GORMAN, T.P. AND HUTCHISON, D. (forthcoming). Study of parents' attitudes and children's scores in NCDS.

GORMAN, T.P. AND MOSS, N. (1979). *Survey of Attainment and Progress of Learners in Adult Literacy Schemes*. Unpublished report to the Department of Education and Science. Slough: NFER.

HANNON, P. (1995). *Literacy, Home and School: research and practice in teaching literacy with parents*. Chichester: Falmer.

HANNON, P., NUTBROWN, C. AND WEINBERGER, J. (1990). *Ways of Working with Parents to Promote Early Literacy Development*. Sheffield: University of Sheffield.

HAYES, A.E. (undated). Hawai'i Family Literacy Pilot Project. Summary Report. 1990-93 and Interim Follow up. Mimeograph.

KAMBOURI, M. AND FRANCIS, H. (1994). *Time to Leave? Progression and drop out in basic skills programmes*. London: Adult Literacy and Basic Skills Unit.

MACLEOD, D. (1995). 'A family affair.' Report, April, 13.

NATIONAL CENTER FOR FAMILY LITERACY (undated). *The Power of Family Literacy*. Louisville, KY: NCFL.

NICKSE, R. (1993). 'A typology of family and intergenerational literacy programs: implications for evaluation.' *Viewpoints 15: Family Literacy*. London: Adult Literacy and Basic Skills Unit, 34-40. (ERIC Document Reproduction Service no. ED 333 166)

NICKSE, R. AND QUEZADA, S. (1994). 'Collaborations: a key to success in Family Literacy programs.' In D.K. Dickinson (ed.) *Bridges to Literacy: children, families, and schools*. Cambridge, MA and Oxford: Blackwell, 211-35.

PARATORE, J.R. (1995). 'Implementing an intergenerational literacy project: lessons learned.' In L.M. Morrow (ed.) *Family Literacy: connections in schools and communities*. Newark, DE: International Reading Association, 37-53.

RODGERS, B. (1986). 'Change in the reading attainment of adults: a longitudinal study', *British Journal of Developmental Psychology*, **4**, 1, 1-17.

SNOW, C.E. (1994). 'Enhancing literacy development: programs and research perspectives.' In D.K. Dickinson (ed.) *Bridges to Literacy: children, families, and schools*. Cambridge, MA and Oxford: Blackwell, 267-72.

ST. PIERRE, R., LAYZER, J. AND BARNES, H. (1994). Variation in the design, cost, and effectiveness of two-generation programs. Paper presented at Eighth Rutgers Invitational Symposium on Education: New Directions for Policy and Research in Early Childhood Care and Education, Princeton, NJ, October 27-28.

ST. PIERRE, R., SWARTZ, J., GAMSE, B., MURRAY, S., DECK., D AND NICKEL, P. (1995). *National Evaluation of the Even Start Family Literacy Program. Final report*. Washington, DC: US Department of Education.

SYLVA, K. AND HURRY, J. (1995). *Early Intervention in Children with Reading Difficulties: an evaluation of Reading Recovery and a phonological training. Full report*. London: School Curriculum and Assessment Authority.

TAYLOR, D. (1983). *Family Literacy*. London: Heinemann.

TOPPING, K. AND WOLFENDALE, S. (1995). 'The effectiveness of family literacy programmes.' *Reading*, **29**, 3, 26-33.

WEINBERGER, J. (1995). 'Parents' contribution to children's literacy learning.' In B. Raban-Bisby, G. Brooks and S. Wolfendale (eds) *Developing Language and Literacy in the English National Curriculum*. Stoke-on-Trent: Trentham Books for UK Reading Association.

Full description of the evaluation

———

A brief description of the evaluation is given in chapter 4. This appendix gives a fuller description of how the evaluation was carried out, shows the extent to which it met its targets for data collection, and discusses a number of technical issues which arose during it.

A.1 Forms of information

It was anticipated that evidence of gain from the Programmes might emerge in:

- *participating parents and/or their children*

- *performance in and/or attitudes towards literacy*

- *activities in the programme and/or at home and/or at school*

- *the short and/or the longer term.*

The evaluation was designed to gather varying amounts of information on all these aspects from a range of interested groups, to collect quantitative and/or qualitative data on these aspects as appropriate, and to complement the evaluative work that was required of the Programmes in any case.

The specific forms of evidence collected by NFER were as shown in Table A.1.

Table A.1: **Forms of evidence collected**

Quantitative data:			
on parents:	background information reading attainment writing attainment literacy activities undertaken at home with children	on children:	background information vocabulary development early reading development early writing development
Qualitative data:			
interviews with parents interviews with Programme Coordinators		observations of teaching sessions teachers' impressions.	

In addition, the Programme Coordinators supplied NFER with their termly reports to the Agency, with information on parents' attendance, retention, accreditation and destinations, and with a great deal of other relevant information and documentation.

A.2 Frequency of data collection

A.2.1 Quantitative data

Background information on parents and children was gathered once, near the beginning of the course.

All the other forms of quantitative data were gathered both near the beginning and just before the end of the course for each of the four termly cohorts of participants. Also, where possible within the timescale of the evaluation, quantitative data were collected 12 weeks and nine months after the end of the course.

This produced the pattern of occasions of quantitative data collection shown in Table A.2.

Table A.2: **Occasions of quantitative data collection**

Cohort	Occasion of data collection	Approximate date
Summer 1994	beginning of course end of course 12-week follow-up 9-month follow-up	April 1994 June 1994 September 1994 April 1995
Autumn 1994	beginning of course end of course 12-week follow-up 9-month follow-up	September 1994 December 1994 March 1995 September 1995
Spring 1995	beginning of course end of course 12-week follow-up	January 1995 March 1995 June 1995
Summer 1995	beginning of course end of course	April 1995 June 1995

Thus across the four cohorts there were 11 occasions on which quantitative data were gathered, including three 12-week and two 9-month follow-ups. All quantitative data were gathered on NFER's behalf by Programme staff.

A.2.2 Qualitative data

Interviews with parents took place towards the end of each course, and on each follow-up occasion. Interviews with coordinators and observations of teaching sessions took place each term. Teachers' impressions were gathered in the spring and summer terms of 1995 only.

A.3 Quantitative data-collection instruments

A.3.1 Background information

Background information on parents was collected through an Adult Profile form covering sex, date of birth, ethnic group, first and any other languages, occupation, highest qualification and whether the parent had been on adult basic skills courses before. A similar Child Profile form covered sex, date of birth, ethnic group and languages. Information on family structures was not collected. Both Profiles are reproduced in Appendix C.

A.3.2 Parents' literacy

Reading

To provide an estimate of their reading attainment, parents were asked on each occasion to complete a three-part cloze test. The texts used, and the deletions, had been devised by the Programmes and the Agency, and agreed by the NFER team. All three tests are reproduced in Appendix D; where the gaps occurred in the versions seen by parents, Appendix D shows the target word in brackets below the gap.

The difficulty level of the first two parts of the cloze test was keyed to the Foundation level of the Agency's Communication Standards, and that of the third test to level 1. These levels were also the basis of the City and Guilds Wordpower accreditation system which was used during the courses. Across the set of three tests, the difficulty of the cloze texts was pitched to be appropriate to the fairly wide range of ability levels expected in the target group.

The content of the texts was designed to be very familiar to the parents (two were about children's early development, the other a letter to parents from a school about a trip).

Marking was carried out on a verbatim basis, that is only the exact word deleted was accepted as correct. 'Synonym' scoring, that is accepting words which gave the same sense and fitted the syntactic context, was not used. This was partly because it is less easy to maintain consistency in marking over different occasions when judgments of the acceptability of alternative answers have to be made; and partly because inspection of early scripts showed that the level of accuracy was in any case rather high. Each deletion was counted as one item, and scores were calculated as the number correct.

Writing

To provide an estimate of their writing attainment, parents were asked on each occasion to complete a three-part writing task. The writing task for the beginning of the term required parents to write their name and address, the names and dates of birth of their children, and short answers to these questions:

- Please write about why you are interested in the course.

- What are some of the things you hope to get from the course?

- Please write a few lines about your children.

The writing task for the end of the term required parents to write short answers to these questions:

- What do you think you have gained from the course?

- Please write about any changes you have seen in your children.

- Have there been any changes in what you do at home with your children, whilst you have been on the course? Please write about this.

The tasks at the two follow-up occasions were identical to each other, and asked parents to respond to these three questions:

- Looking back on the course what would you say were the main things you got from it?

- Please write about any changes you have seen in your children since the course finished.

- Please write about some of the things you and your children have done since the course finished.

The scripts were first assessed holistically (impressionistically) on a rising 7-point scale (1 = low, 7 = high) which reflected the range of performance in the sample as a whole. A script was assigned to category 1 only if the adult concerned had written only his/her name and address and children's names (on pp.1-2 of the initial task), or less. Such instances were rare, in this sample. In Figure A.1 on the following six pages are reproduced six complete 12-week follow-up scripts (p.3c). They illustrate in turn the range of performance from category 2 to category 7.

124

Figure A.1: **Example of parents' writing, stages 2-7**

Stage 2

1. Looking back on the course what would you say were the main things you got from it:

> Learning to Spell.
> but Learing lot More.

2. Please write about any changes you have seen in your children since the course finished:

> they have came out of they
> ~~Sta~~ talking more to people

3. Please write about some of the things you and your children have done since the course finished:

> make thing at home
> with them.

Stage 3

1. Looking back on the course what would you say were the main things you got from it:

I got alot of help out of the course.
and alot more comfident in my self.

2. Please write about any changes you have seen in your children since the course finished:

I have seen a lot of Diffrents in my
Children since they have finished the
course.

3. Please write about some of the things you and your children have done since the course finished:

We have Done alot of Reading
and writing with the children.
and makenng all Diffrent things.

Stage 4

1. Looking back on the course what would you say were the main things you got from it:

Confidence in myself. more patience with the children. A better understanding to the needs of the children.

2. Please write about any changes you have seen in your children since the course finished:

The children will now ask me to help them with activities at home, they know I now have more patience with them than before.

3. Please write about some of the things you and your children have done since the course finished:

We have done sticking at home and made books together. As well as painting and play acting

---

Stage 5

1. Looking back on the course what would you say were the main things you got from it:

   I learned how important it is to help your child to read and write and not just leave it to the school. I learnt different ways to help them. It also built mine and my childrens confidence about learning.

2. Please write about any changes you have seen in your children since the course finished:

   My children can both draw better pictures instead of scribbling they are more confident. They try and write. Also my daughters speech has got better since doing the course.

3. Please write about some of the things you and your children have done since the course finished:

   when I have moved I intend to do some further education courses. They have started school and nursery and are getting on well.

Stage 6

1. Looking back on the course what would you say were the main things you
   got from it:

   It helped me build up my self ~~confif~~
   confidence and helped me make up my mind
   what I wanted to do next.

2. Please write about any changes you have seen in your children since the
   course finished:

   I've seen a change in the way that my
   daughter will sit with me and try and
   read books.

3. Please write about some of the things you and your children have done
   since the course finished:

   I have now gone on to do the wordpower
   Stage 2 and the number power stage 1
   and I am also doing a child development G.C.So
   with my daughter I do a lot more reading
   and writing.

Stage 7

1. Looking back on the course what would you say were the main things you got from it:

The course made me realize that although my children are very important to me I need to think about myself and what I want to do and not to feel selfish for doing things I want to do. Before the course my life revolved around my family and housework. Now I have realized that I deserve to reserve some time for myself to do what I want

2. Please write about any changes you have seen in your children since the course finished:

Paul will tell you some things about what he has done at school. Before the course he very rarely told me what he'd done at school. He asks me to do sums for him and he likes using the abacus to do them.

3. Please write about some of the things you and your children have done since the course finished:

In the summer holidays me made a scrap book on what we'd done and where we'd been. We done this together. Paul would draw the pictures and I would do the writing. Paul asks me to do sums for him Paul's handwriting has improved as he was having difficulty with being left handed.

In addition to the impression mark, the number of lines in the parents' scripts was counted, and the scripts were assessed according to a detailed analytic scheme, which is reproduced in the Annex to this Appendix. Briefly, it encompassed:

- *a set of linguistic categories covering formal features of writing (knowledge of orthographic conventions, including spelling; knowledge of grammatical conventions; knowledge of stylistic conventions in written English; handwriting)*

- *a set of detailed content categories.*

The analysis according to linguistic categories was used as background to the general impression marking, and the main findings are reported in the section on parents' writing attainment in chapter 8. Part of that analysis was based on an error/length ratio calculated by:

- *adding together the number of errors in the grammar and style categories*

- *dividing that total by the number of lines written.*

This ratio was calculated because the scripts parents produced at the end of term and at follow-ups tended to be considerably longer than those from the beginning of the term. To have reported raw numbers of errors would therefore have produced the misleading impression that parents were making more frequent errors at later stages than at the start.

The content analysis was based on the coding schemes. Separate categories were devised for scripts from the beginning and end of the course and from follow-ups (since the task was the same at both follow-ups, the same coding scheme was used for both). Findings from the content analysis are used in this report not as evidence on parents' *attainment*, but as further evidence (supplementing the parent interviews) on parents' *opinions*. Such findings will therefore be found wherever relevant, and not in the sections concerned with parents' writing attainment.

A.3.3 Literacy-related home activities

Information on home literacy activities was gathered mainly through a structured questionnaire which parents completed in an interview with a Programme Coordinator. The questionnaire is reproduced in Appendix B, with the data. The questionnaire consisted of 35 items, all but two answered on a six-point scale. For 33 of the items the response scale was 'Never – once or twice a year – once or twice a month – once a week – two or three times a week – every day'.

It might be objected that responses to such a questionnaire would show only what parents thought the desired answers should be. This objection is undermined by two features of the findings:

> • *the answers to some items where no 'desired response' is feasible (e.g. frequency of reading religious material with children) fitted into a plausible pattern with the rest*

> • *the trend in the answers over time could not have been produced by second-guessing.*

A picture of literacy-related home activities before participation was given in chapter 5, and changes in the pattern were discussed in chapter 7.

To supplement the questionnaire information, in interviews with parents during the courses a few graded questions of a similar nature were used. These results are also reported in chapter 7.

A.3.4 Children's vocabulary and literacy development

Information on children's vocabulary, reading and writing was gathered for NFER by the Early Years Coordinators.

Writing

For 'writing', they asked the children to produce a few lines or a sentence if they could, or if not their own name and some other letters, or if not that then letter-like forms or scribbles, or if not that then a copy of a few words, or if not that then a drawing. The objective was to elicit at each stage the most advanced form of emergent or early writing which the child could produce independently.

Vocabulary and reading

For vocabulary and reading, the tests used were respectively the *Peabody Picture Vocabulary Test – Revised, Form L*, and the *Reading Recognition subtest* of the *Peabody Individual Achievement Tests*. These United States tests are referred to in this report as the PPVT and PIAT respectively, and jointly as the 'Peabody tests'. The PPVT was used in the slightly anglicised version devised for and used in the fifth sweep of the National Child Development Study (NCDS) in 1992. The PIAT was also used on that occasion. All four Early Years Coordinators, and five of their Early Years colleagues, were trained in the use of both tests by Dr Peter Shepherd and Dr Kate Smith of the Social Statistics Research Unit at City University, London, who were involved in NCDS and trained the testers for that study.

The leader of the NFER evaluation also took part in the training sessions, and observed part of the first administration of the Peabody tests by the Early Years

Coordinators. His presence at some of the early assessments was intended to help ensure that the coordinators were administering the tests both in accordance with the instructions and therefore consistently with each other. He was satisfied from his observations that a good level of reliability was being achieved.

In the PPVT test, the child is asked to indicate which of four pictures corresponds to the word the tester has spoken. Scores on this test therefore provide a measure of 'passive' (listening) vocabulary. For the children in this study, no test data were gathered on other aspects of their speaking abilities − for this, evidence was drawn from what their parents wrote, and said in interviews.

A.4 Control group issues

A.4.1 The Peabody tests as a control group device

The Peabody tests were chosen as being the most appropriate available tests to use with the children involved in this initiative and for the purposes of this evaluation. An important objective of the Family Literacy initiative was to boost the literacy attainment of the children of parents whose own literacy attainment was low, in order that those children would have the chance to break out of the intergenerational cycle of low literacy and attainment levels. To demonstrate that the initiative was achieving this aim, it was necessary to show not only that Programme staff, parents and teachers (or even the evaluators) **believed** that children were benefiting, but also that the benefit was actually showing up in children's **attainment**. Information on what the various groups believed was also necessary, but as context for the attainment data, and as part of the explanation of any measured improvement in attainment.

In order to investigate whether children's attainment has improved, it is necessary to test them. But the type of test is crucial. It is not enough to test before an intervention, re-test after it and show a gain, since that would be expected simply from the passage of time, from the fact that the children are growing and learning. What is needed is a demonstration that the improvement is **significantly greater than would be expected simply because the children are older by the time of the post-test.**

To show this, it would again not be enough to show that children had made gains and that their teachers and testers **believed** that they had made greater-than-expected progress. What is needed is an empirical, quantitative demonstration that the gains are significantly greater than those achieved by comparable children who had not received the special treatment, but who were receiving 'normal' treatment, both in the sense that they were growing but also in the sense that they (or some of them) were experiencing the 'normal' curriculum in school.

This can be investigated only if there is a control or reference group for whom data are available showing 'normal' progress, the amount of improvement that can be expected simply because the children are some months older by the time of the post-test. For children of the ages involved in this initiative (three to six years) the **only** tests for which such data were available in Britain at the time were the Peabody tests, and the data arose from the use of those tests in NCDS. Even then, no data existed for children under the age of 4 years 0 months (4:00), since the test would not have been suitable for children so young, and three-year-olds were therefore not tested in NCDS. For children aged 4:00-4:11, data existed only on the PPVT. For those aged 5:00-6:11, data existed on both tests.

In this evaluation, therefore, children aged 3:00-3:11 at the beginning of the course were not tested (though emergent writing samples were gathered from some), those aged 4:00-4:11 at that point were tested only on the PPVT, and those aged 5:00-6:11 were tested on both the PPVT and the PIAT. Children tested at the beginning of a course were tested again on the same instrument(s) at the end of the course and, where the evaluation design called for it, at one or both of the follow-ups. Children who were not tested at the beginning of a course were not tested later even if they turned four during the course; similarly, children tested only on the PPVT at the beginning of a course continued to be tested only on that part of the Peabody tests, and not on the PIAT, even if they turned five during the course. This is because it would not have been useful to have later test data on children for whom no baseline (beginning of course) measure existed.

Some of the children who had been nearly seven when first tested at the beginning of a course were nearly eight by the time of the 9-month follow-ups (which occurred nine months after the *end* of the Summer and Autumn 1994 courses and therefore 12 months after the beginning of them). The standardisation data from NCDS allowed for this, however, since norms for both Peabody tests could be calculated up to (and well beyond) the age of 8:00.

It should be pointed out that, each time they were tested, individual children were compared with a different set of children from NCDS. Consider, for instance, children in this evaluation aged 5:00 at the beginning of a course. Their scores would be standardised against the scores of children in NCDS who had been 5:00 at the time of NCDS. The children in this evaluation aged 5:00 at the beginning of a course would be aged, on average, 5:03 at the end of the course; and their scores then would be standardised against the scores of children in NCDS who had been 5:03 at the time of NCDS, that is, a different set of children. But if both sets of children in NCDS were nationally representative, this would not affect the reliability of the standardisation procedure used here, and the NCDS data could therefore be confidently used as a measure of 'expected' progress.

The PPVT was used in a similar way in connection with three intergenerational family literacy programmes in the United States:

> • *in the evaluation of a pilot family literacy project in Hawai'i (Hayes, undated)*

> • *by the National Center for Family Literacy (undated) in its evaluation of one of its own programmes, Toyota Families for Learning, and*

> • *in the national evaluation of Even Start (St Pierre et al., 1995).*

Some comparative PPVT data from these evaluations are reported in chapter 6.

No test of significance was reported by Hayes (undated) for the Hawai'i result mentioned in chapter 6. In the Even Start evaluation, children in a control group who (officially) received no extra provision at all made similar gains to those in the programme (St. Pierre *et al*, 1995, p.169-71). Moreover, St. Pierre *et al.* (1994, p.15) pointed out that the NCFL study contained no (specially selected) control group, and therefore discounted its finding in the light of the Even Start control group result. This might lead to some reservations about the PPVT data from the United States.

However, the Even Start samples were rather small for a 'national' evaluation – 76 and 70 in the 'experimental' group and the control group respectively (St. Pierre *et al*, 1995, p.171). Also, it may be that the parents of the control group children, knowing that their children were in a research study and were going to be re-tested, somehow increased their children's early literacy experiences in a way which had an equal effect to Even Start; this would greatly reduce the validity of using these children as a control group. And it seems erroneous to argue that the NCFL study had no control group – as argued above, the children on whom the national standardisations of the PPVT were based **are** a control group, and both a larger and therefore more reliable one than the 70 children in the Even Start evaluation. Therefore the view is taken here that the improvements on the PPVT in the US studies were more significant than St. Pierre *et al.* considered them to be.

A.4.2 Representativeness of the NCDS samples

There was one respect in which the representativeness of the samples of children in NCDS might be queried, namely whether their parents were a nationally representative sample in the first place. Here, 'nationally representative' would mean 'nationally representative of parents of children aged 3:00-6:11'. But all the cohort members in the 1992 NCDS study were by definition aged 33 at the time, and in this respect only they were a less representative sample than the parents in this evaluation, whose age-range was much wider (see Figure 5.1).

On the other hand, in other respects the NCDS sample was more representative than the parents in this evaluation. In particular, half the cohort members in NCDS were men, compared to four per cent here, and the full NCDS sample undoubtedly represented a much wider socioeconomic and educational range (see section 5.1) than the parents in this evaluation, thus virtually guaranteeing that the initial mean scores of the children here would be much lower. Furthermore, it has been suggested by those who conducted NCDS (Bynner, personal communication) that poorer and less qualified cohort members had a greater tendency to drop out of that study; this would tend to exaggerate the difference between NCDS and evaluation children, by pushing the average raw scores of the children in NCDS up, and therefore the average standardised scores of the children in this evaluation down.

In order to compare the two groups of children more directly, a series of progressively more narrowly defined subsamples of NCDS parents were selected, and their children's average PPVT and PIAT scores calculated:

- *the first calculation was based on the children of all NCDS cohort members (men and women) who had at least one child aged between 3:00 and 6:11*

- *next, only mothers were selected (but since there were few fathers in the Family Literacy sample, they were not taken out of that sample for this comparison)*

- *then, only monolingual English speakers were selected. This and the other re-samplings also had the effect of removing from the sample all but a few mothers from ethnic minorities – and since there were also very few parents from ethnic minorities in the Family Literacy sample those remaining in the NCDS sample were **not** excluded from this calculation*

- *fourthly, only those with no O-Levels or equivalent were selected*

- *finally, only those not employed outside the home were selected (see the definition of 'At home' in section 5.1).*

The resulting mean scores on the Peabody tests for these subsamples' children are shown in Table A.3, with the beginning-of-course scores of the Family Literacy children for comparison.

Thus, even when a group of NCDS children was selected to be as closely matched as the data allowed on their parents' characteristics, that group's average scores were significantly higher than those of the Family Literacy children at the beginning of the course. This further emphasised the gap between the Family Literacy children's starting point and the skills of the mass of children of the same ages.

Table A.3: **Peabody test scores for NCDS subsamples**

Parent subsample	Children's scores					
	PPVT			PIAT		
	N	mean score	(s.d.)	N	mean score	(s.d.)
All cohort members	2385	99.9	(14.9)	2617	99.8	(14.8)
Mothers only	952	101.8	(14.9)	1127	100.7	(14.1)
Monolinguals only	920	101.7	(14.9)	1089	100.6	(14.1)
Without qualifications	296	95.9	(15.8)	377	96.6	(14.2)
Those 'at home'	110	95.7	(16.7)	149	93.2	(13.8)
Family Literacy	330	84.8	(13.0)	180	83.6	(16.2)

Key: N = sample size;   s.d. = standard deviation

A.4.3 The control group issue for other quantitative data

No control group data of any sort existed for any of the other forms of quantitative data gathered in this evaluation, since no appropriate instruments had yet been standardised. This meant that the 'standard' rate of progress in writing for children of this age-range (or indeed for older children), or for adults on any of the measures taken here, was not known.

However, if significant growth occurred in children's writing alongside significant improvement in their vocabulary and reading, it would be highly unlikely that this could arise from a separate, unrelated cause.

For adults, age-standardised tests of reading and writing do not exist, and probably cannot, since 'standard progress to be expected of adults at particular ages' is a psychologically bizarre notion. However, there is a little research evidence to suggest that adults of the main age-range in this initiative might be expected to make a small amount of progress. In 1961, a nationally representative sample of 15-year-olds in Britain took a reading test; in 1972, now aged 26, just over 3,000 of them took the same test again (for full details, see Rodgers, 1986). The results showed a small but significant improvement in the average score. More recently, in 1993 separate nationally representative samples of adults aged 22-24, 32-34, and so on up to 72-74 took a reading test (different from that used in the 1961/72 study). The results (see ALBSU, 1995) showed an increase in average scores from 22-24 up to 42-44, then no difference up to 62-64, then a fall. It is logically possible that those aged between 42 and 64 in the ALBSU study had left school with higher average attainments than the younger samples had and that no group's average had changed since, but both the lower score of the over-seventies and the longitudinal 1961/72 study make this unlikely. The most parsimonious explanation of the two sets of results is that young adults continue to improve their reading skills after leaving school, that a plateau is reached in middle age, and that decline sets in in later years.

If so, then it would be expected that adults of the main age-range in this study would make a certain amount of progress. But that amount would be tiny. The samples in the 1993 study were a decade apart in age, and the 1961/72 group aged 11 years between the two testings. The absolute differences in average scores were not large in either case, and if scaled down to what would be 'expected' over a period of 10-11 **weeks** would be minute. Sheer lapse of time would therefore not be a probable explanation of any gains made by parents in this study.

However, even if the children involved in this evaluation did show a greater than expected gain in performance in vocabulary and reading, and both they and their parents showed significant improvement in other quantitative measures, such findings on their own could be attributed either to the specifics of the intervention, or more simply to the greatly increased amount of expert attention they were receiving (a form of 'Hawthorn effect'). It was not possible to design this study in such a way as to eliminate this ambiguity rigorously. This would have required the setting up of a control group who received a 'different but equal' intervention, and such a design would not have been practicable, either financially or conceptually – the latter because it would have been virtually impossible to define what a 'different but equal' intervention should consist of. Rather, the explanations, both for the Peabody findings and for the other forms of quantitative data, were teased apart with the aid of the other forms of data which were collected, and in this context the qualitative information was central.

A.5 Qualitative data collection

Interviews with parents during the courses were conducted by three NFER researchers, one covering Cardiff, another Liverpool and North Tyneside, and the Project Leader Norfolk. Follow-up interviews with parents after the course were conducted mainly by the Programmes' Adult Coordinators. The interviews were based on semi-structured interview schedules (these are reproduced in Appendix E). The schedule used during the courses covered how parents came to hear about the Programme, why they joined, what they saw as the benefits to themselves and their children, what they had learnt for themselves and for helping their children, and what they planned to do afterwards. The schedule used at follow-up occasions covered how parents' plans had worked out, the extent to which the benefits were continuing, and general comments.

The interviews with Programme Coordinators (both Adult and Early Years) were also based on semi-structured schedules (reproduced in Appendix F), and were conducted by the NFER researchers. The schedules were different in each term, and evolved to cover the different stages of the initiative and emerging issues. Broadly, the issues covered were the initial stages of the Programme, recruitment, teaching (both approach and content), the coordinators' own opinions of the effectiveness of various aspects of the Programmes, how they kept in touch with past groups, relationships with 'host' schools (including any feedback on children who had been in a Programme), premises, staffing, resources, the Agency's model of family literacy, benefit to parents and children, and prospects for continuing the work after the end of the pilot Programmes.

Observations of teaching sessions were carried out by the NFER researchers using a schedule (see Appendix G) which covered discussions with the tutor before and after the session, log-keeping during it, and judgments reached on the basis of this information.

The system used for gathering teachers' impressions was small-scale. It operated during the spring and summer terms 1995, and covered one or two children per Programme per term. Each Early Years Coordinator was asked to speak to an infants teacher in her Programme's 'host' school, to identify with her one or two children who would be moving into that school from the Programme, and to ask the teacher to make intermittent observations on those children during one term and complete a brief questionnaire about them at the end of the term (see Appendix H).

A.6 Targets for data collection

The target for background information on parents and children was to gather it only at the beginning of the course, but on all recruited parents and their qualifying children, i.e. those aged between 3:00 and 6:11 at that point.

The target for all other forms of quantitative information was to gather such data:

- *at the beginning of the course, on all recruited parents and their qualifying children*

- *at the end of the course, on all the parents who completed a course and on their participating children*

- *at follow-ups, on all parents who agreed to re-visit their Programme and on their participating children.*

The targets for qualitative information were:

- *to interview 10 parents in each Programme during the first three terms of the evaluation, five in each Programme during the summer term of 1995 (total: 140), and as many as possible of these parents again at relevant follow-ups*

- *to interview each Adult Coordinator and each Early Years Coordinator (10 people in all because of two job-shares) once per term (total number of interviews: 40)*

- *to observe one parents-only teaching session, one children-only session, and one joint session per Programme per term (total number of observations: 48, 16 of each type of session)*

- *to gather teachers' impressions, in the spring and summer terms of 1995 only, on one or two children who moved from each of the Programmes into primary school (maximum: 16).*

A.7 Quantitative data collected: parents

A summary of the quantitative data collected on parents is shown in Table A.4.

Table A.4: **Summary of quantitative data collected on parents, by cohort**

Cohort	Summer 1994	Autumn 1994	Spring 1995	Summer 1995	Total
Number of adult profiles returned at start of course	68	103	102	88	361
Number of parents tested at					
– start of course	68	97	108	93	366
– end of course	59	79	92	79	309
– 12-week follow-up	49	70	69	n/a	188
– 9-month follow-up	34	54	n/a	n/a	88

The figures for parents tested are the overall numbers, those for whom at least one piece of test information was returned. For the first and second of the three cloze (reading) tests in particular, the numbers tended to be smaller (see sections 5.3 and 8.1).

On average, the proportion of parents tested at the beginning of term who were re-tested at the end was 85 per cent. Information on retention rates provided by the Programmes showed that **91 per cent of parents who were recruited onto courses completed them**; if those who completed courses are used as the basis for calculation then the proportion who were re-tested at the end was 93 per cent. Retention rates in ordinary Adult Basic Skills courses are typically much lower than this, although it should be borne in mind that provision is frequently on a 'drop in' or open learning basis. For example, Kambouri and Francis (1994, p.8) found that 'Half of the students enrolled during 1991-92 were reported to have left classes at some time during the year'. The high completion and re-test rates on the Programmes betoken powerful motivation on these parents' part to complete.

Reasons for non-completion, where it occurred, were collected by the Programmes. The main one was a change in the shifts or hours of part-time work. There were also a few cases each of medical reasons (including a few births), younger children not settling in the crèche, and students moving out of the area.

Table A.4 also shows, as might be expected, some 'attrition' (falling-off in numbers) in the samples after the courses had ended, particularly between the two follow-ups. The proportion of those tested at the end of the first three terms who were re-tested at 12-week follow-up was 82 per cent (or 70 per cent of those tested at the beginning); and the proportion of those tested at 12-week follow-up after the first two terms who were re-tested at 9-month follow-up was 75 per cent (or 64 per cent of those tested at the end of the course, or 55 per cent of those tested at the beginning). However, for a medium-term study of this sort, what is remarkable here is not how many parents did not return for testing on later occasions, but how many did return; follow-up participation rates are typically much lower. The effect of attrition on the reliability of the test data is discussed in section A.9 on page 142.

A.8 Quantitative data collected: children

A summary of the quantitative data collected on children is shown in Table A.5 on the next page.

Attrition in this sample was of course very similar to that in the sample of parents. The numbers of children tested at the start of the courses were lower than the numbers for whom child profiles were returned; this is because no child aged under 4:00 at the start of a course was tested at any point. But again, the figures for children tested are the overall numbers, and the numbers who were tested on the PIAT were considerably lower (see sections 5.5 and 6.2), because only children aged over 5:00 at the start of a course were given that test.

Table A.5: **Summary of quantitative data collected on children, by cohort**

Cohort	Summer 1994	Autumn 1994	Spring 1995	Summer 1995	Total
Number of child profiles returned at start of course	77	106	112	97	392
Number of children tested at					
– start of course	71	92	116	96	375
– end of course	66	75	95	80	316
– 12-week follow-up	64	75	82	n/a	221
– 9-month follow-up	59	66	n/a	n/a	125

A.9 The effect of sample attrition on performance data: using only returners rather than all test-takers

In chapters 6 and 8, comparisons of children's and parents' test performances at different stages are made on the basis of 'returners' only. To use the data from all those who took the test at each stage would be misleading, for two reasons.

First, the numbers of cohorts involved were not the same at all stages, and the 9-month follow-up (for example) should therefore be compared with previous stages only for the two cohorts involved. However, if comparisons were based only on those who were tested on all four occasions, the data from the last two cohorts would not be analysed at all. The 12-week follow-up should be compared with previous stages for the three cohorts involved, and the end of course result should be compared with the beginning of course result for all four cohorts.

Secondly, the subsamples of parents who returned for testing at each later stage were 'self-selected' (only those who were willing to be re-tested came back, and the rest stayed away), and the subsamples of children who returned were, in effect, selected by their parents. There is the possibility that those parents who had lower initial scores might have had a greater tendency not to return for re-testing; in other words, that there might have been 'differential attrition'. And this in turn might have pushed the later average scores up, artificially. Similarly, if non-returning parents' children also tended to have lower initial scores, those children's absence on later occasions might have caused the children's mean scores to rise artificially. And in fact, the results given in chapters 6 and 8 did show that a certain amount of biasing from differential attrition had occurred in both the parent and the child data.

To overcome these difficulties, the test data in those chapters were presented in a way which allowed the results for those tested at each stage to be compared with the results from earlier stages for *only the same people*, that is, only for *returners*. In this way, the different numbers of cohorts were allowed for, and differences which arose genuinely from improvements by the people concerned could be distinguished from differences which might have arisen spuriously from differential attrition.

However, another check needed to be made before the test data for returners only could be presented as reliable. If the numbers of returners at any stage were too small a proportion of all those who had taken the test then, they might be an unrepresentative subsample. The information for making this check is presented in Table A.6. The Table shows, separately for each cloze test, for parents' writing, for the two Peabody tests and for children's writing, the total numbers of people who returned for testing at each stage after the beginning of the course and, alongside, the numbers within that who had also been tested at all relevant previous occasions – that is, the number of 'returners' for that test for that occasion. The number of returners is also shown as a percentage of the relevant full number of test-takers.

Table A.6: Parents and children tested on each occasion: numbers of all test-takers and of returners compared

	End of course			12-week follow-up			9-month follow-up		
	N1	N2	%	N1	N2	%	N1	N2	%
Parents									
Cloze test 1	147	142	97%	80	80	100%	38	28	74%
Cloze test 2	176	170	97%	94	91	97%	43	35	81%
Cloze test 3	302	282	94%	183	161	88%	66	55	83%
Writing	302	251	83%	182	151	83%	87	56	64%
Children									
PPVT	291	273	94%	215	192	89%	120	112	93%
PIAT	187	147	79%	155	101	65%	80	67	84%
Writing	304	279	92%	216	179	83%	109	91	83%

Key: N1 = number of all test-takers
N2 = number of returners (cf. Tables 6.1, 6.2, 6.3, 8.1 and 8.2)
% = returners as a percentage of all test-takers

Thus the number of returners as a percentage of all test-takers was over 80 per cent, and entirely satisfactory, in all but two cases. Since the two exceptions, 64 and 65 per cent, were not ideal, it was decided that no claim to a significant result should be based on them. This had rather little effect, since:

> • *the result for parents' writing at 9-month follow-up was in any case non-significant*

> • *the result for the PIAT at 12-week follow-up was either non-significant or, where significant, was backed by significant results based on other occasions of testing (see discussion following Table 6.2).*

All test results in chapters 6 and 8 based on returners only and claimed as significant were therefore calculated on a reliable percentage of all test-takers.

A.10 Quantitative data collected: literacy-related home activities

The numbers of Home Activities questionnaires returned are shown in Table A.7.

Table A.7: **Numbers of Home Activities questionnaires completed, by cohort**

Cohort	Summer 1994	Autumn 1994	Spring 1995	Summer 1995	Total
Number of questionnaires returned at					
– start of course	70	108	117	101	396
– end of course	62	81	97	83	323
– 12-week follow-up	52	73	77	n/a	202
– 9-month follow-up	35	58	n/a	n/a	93

In addition, of the 132 parents who were interviewed during the courses, 111 answered five questions on the frequency of and changes in home literacy-related activities.

A.11 Qualitative data collected

A summary of the qualitative data collected is shown in Table A.8.

Table A.8: **Summary of qualitative data collected, by cohort**

Cohort	Summer 1994	Autumn 1994	Spring 1995	Summer 1995	Total
Number of parents interviewed					
– during course	32	39	35	17	123
– at 12-week follow-up	24	31	24	n/a	79
– at 9-month follow-up	15	21	n/a	n/a	36
Number of interviews with Programme Coordinators	9	10	9	8	36
Number of observations of					
– parents-only sessions	6	4	4	4	18
– children-only sessions	4	4	5	6	19
– joint sessions	4	5	4	4	17
Total	14	13	13	14	54
Number of children on whom teachers' impressions were gathered					
	n/a	n/a	5	8	13

Attrition is again noticeable in the parental interviews. It should be remembered that only a subsample of parents was interviewed in any term, and that by design teachers' impressions were gathered on only a very small number of children.

A.12 Comments on data collection

The forms of information collected from parents comprised:

> • *three cloze tests, a writing task and a Home Activities questionnaire, collected from all or most parents, at the beginning and end of the course and at follow-ups*

> • *interviews with some parents, both during the course (including further questions on home literacy-related activities) and at follow-ups.*

The total amount of information collected from parents might be seen as burdensome. However, the assessment instruments and methodology were worked through at one of the Programme Coordinators' residential seminars, in order to achieve a system which was valid, not disruptive of teaching, and understood by all staff. Also, the coordinators acted with great sensitivity and tact in carrying out the assessments, and parents' reactions were positive. Perhaps the best testimony to parents' acceptance of the data collection was the high proportions who returned for re-testing at the end of the course and particularly at the follow-ups.

In terms of the targets set for data collection, the evaluation itself was very successful:

> • *all recruited parents were profiled and tested at the beginning of the course, and at the same stage all their qualifying children were profiled and tested on writing*

> • *all completing parents were tested at the end of the course, and at the same stage all their participating children were again tested on writing*

> • *a satisfactory proportion of parents and children returned for testing at both follow-ups (though not quite for every test)*

> • *at all these stages, all relevant children qualified by age at the beginning of the course to do so were tested on the PPVT and PIAT*

> • *Home Activities questionnaires were completed by all parents tested at each stage*

> • *the number of parents interviewed during the courses (123) was close to the target (140), and satisfactory numbers were re-interviewed at follow-ups (81 and 36 respectively, or 76 per cent and 64 per cent respectively of the relevant samples interviewed at the previous stage)*

> • *the number of interviews with coordinators (36) was close to the target (40)*

> • *the number of observations of teaching sessions (54) was slightly above target (48)*

> • *the number of children on whom teachers' impression were gathered (13) was close to the target (16).*

Coding schemes for analysis of parents' writing

———

1. Linguistic categories

The linguistics-based analytic assessments related to the writer's knowledge of

A Orthography
B Grammatical conventions

C Stylistic conventions
D Handwriting.

For the categories relating to **Orthography, Grammar** and **Style,** the total number of errors within each category was recorded. Handwriting was assessed on a rising 1-3 scale.

1A Orthography

In assigning a mark for this category account was taken of:

a) conventions of spelling and word division

b) capital letters

c) the occurrence of errors in the use of punctuation that did not result in grammatical error as defined below.

a) Conventions of spelling and word division

Spelling errors are of numerous types:

- homophones *(their/there, write/right, knew/new, etc.)*

- 'rational' misspellings, transpositions, omissions, insertions, contractions

- mistakes over doubling of letters, etc.

- 'slips' of various kinds.

Errors in word division often occur in relation to compounds, e.g. *in to, out side,* and through misanalysis of standard forms, e.g. *now days, alot, after noon,* etc.

Word-internal punctuation errors tend to occur in relation to the possessive apostrophe, contracted forms, hyphens in compounds and full stops in abbreviations: *the fathers' quite strict; your/you're; did'nt, wasent,* etc.

Wrongly spelt verb forms (especially past tense) are usually more appropriately dealt with under 'style', when the form given is a close equivalent to a spoken form (e.g. endings with 't' rather than 'ed', 'of' instead of 'have'/'-ve').

b) Conventions of capitalisation

Commonly, this involves a failure to begin a sentence with a capital letter. Relatedly, a capital letter may be given without a full stop or other associated punctuation mark. Proper names and titles may lack capitals.

In some scripts upper and lower case letters are not systematically distinguished. These occurrences are not dealt with as orthographic errors, but are taken account of in relation to the handwriting category, below. This is because learning to distinguish between upper and lower case letters or scripts is a stage that generally precedes the learning of conventions of spelling or capitalisation.

c) Non-grammatical punctuation (not causing ambiguity)

Included in this category are superfluous commas; commas used in place of full stops or colons; errors in speech marks/quotation marks and associated punctuation.

Where orthographic errors of types (b) and (c) are linked to phrase, clause or sentence boundaries they are still counted in this category rather than the next. If, for example, a writer omits a full stop at the end of a sentence but begins the subsequent sentence with a capital letter, it is clear that the sentence boundary is recognised and this would therefore be regarded as an orthographic error, and not as a grammatical error (see next paragraph).

1B Grammatical conventions

A number of conventions are observed by proficient writers which reflect the need to represent unambiguously the relations between the parts of sentences, and clause relations and boundaries. In speech, these relations are indicated in part by patterns of intonation. In writing, they are generally indicated by marks of punctuation; these can be considered grammatical punctuation, as distinct from the non-grammatical punctuation described in the previous section. Where these are not used appropriately, the grammatical relationship between two or more clauses may be unclear or open to more than one interpretation. The grammatical relationship between parts of a sentence may also be misinterpreted if commas are omitted or wrongly placed around phrases in apposition, in a succession of nouns or adjectives, or between clauses and phrases.

Other common grammatical errors are the result of the lack of cohesion or relatedness between different parts of a sentence or between successive clauses, e.g. in maintaining tense sequence in adjacent clauses, or grammatical 'agreement' between components of a sentence, where this is required to prevent ambiguity.

1C Stylistic conventions

In the context of this assessment the term 'style' refers to the writer's choice of appropriate vocabulary and sentence structure, taking account of the subject matter and audience. As writers become more proficient and as their writing repertoire is extended, the incidence of grammatical errors tends to lessen, and the handling of stylistic conventions to become more of an issue.

Some of the stylistic errors in these scripts stem from the use in writing of words or phrases associated with colloquial speech. The elision and lack of formal coherence that are characteristic of informal speech are generally judged to be inappropriate in writing. In this assessment, the use of grammatical features that are characteristic of regional variants of standard English, and the use of colloquial expressions or of slang, are taken into account in relation to the category of style, as is the inappropriate use of non-standard forms such as 'I done it'.

1D Handwriting

In categorising handwriting, the following classifications were used:

1. Handwriting which is difficult to interpret because the writer has difficulty in controlling letter formation

2. Handwriting in which there is general control of letter formation but a lack of systematic distinction between upper and lower case letters

3. Handwriting which is intelligible and systematic.

The great majority of scripts fell into Category 3; very few scripts were allocated to Category 1.

2. Content analysis

On each occasion when parents were asked to undertake the writing task, the resulting scripts displayed a range of interesting ideas and comments. In order to handle the range of content, coding schemes were developed, consisting of a set of content categories, each of which was coded on a present/absent basis. The content categories were arrived at by analyses of the scripts, and the categories represented statements made by at least three adults in their undirected commentaries on the questions asked. The category system was not evaluative; that is to say, there was no implication that any or all of the categories should be referred to by those responding.

The purpose of the categories was simply to record the range and frequency of comments that parents made.

Beginning of course

Of the three questions to which parents are asked to respond at the beginning of the course, the third evoked responses which did not lend themselves to this form of analysis, and the content analysis was therefore restricted to the other two questions. Those two questions in turn did not elicit different types of response, and they were therefore analysed together.

The coding scheme devised for these two questions had five categories relating to the main types of reasons given by parents for their interest in the course and the benefits they hoped to obtain by involvement in it. The categories were as follows:

1. To help their child(ren).

2. To understand how children are taught or learn at school.

3. To improve their own skills.

4. To socialise or meet people.

5. To demonstrate capability.

End of course

In devising the scheme for coding the content of parents' writing at the end of the course it was found that each of the three questions needed to be analysed separately. The categories for the three questions were as follows:

Question 1.
 1. More knowledge about how to help my child in reading
 2. More knowledge about how to help with writing
 3. More knowledge about creative play/how to make toys and games
 4. More understanding of how children learn/what children are taught in school
 5. More patience
 6. More confidence
 7. I am better at reading/I read more
 8. I am better at writing
 9. I know more about computers/wordprocessing
10. I know how to study/to think things through
11. I know how to get further qualifications/I want to further my education
12. I have made new friends/I enjoyed the company of the group

Question 2.

1. The children have learnt letters/phonics/numbers
2. Reading has improved
3. Writing, copying, spelling, handwriting has improved
4. Speaking/listening has improved/children are more outspoken/ask more questions/talk more about school
5. Overall abilities have improved
6. Better attitudes to learning/better motivation/enjoy learning/concentrate more
7. Have more friends/are more sociable
8. More confident/self-reliant/outgoing/independent
9. More creative activities/drawing/cutting and sticking
10. Enjoyed the time together/want more involvement with me/eager for me to join in
11. They gained a lot/improved at school/have come on well

Question 3.

1. (More) reading/sharing books
2. (More) writing/making books/photo-albums/scrapbooks
3. (More) talking/listening/communicating about school
4. (More) creative play/activities including drawing/colouring
5. (More) interaction for learning in daily life
6. (More) patience/understanding/better attitudes and communication
7. We spend more time together

Follow-ups

The coding scheme used for the end of the course was retained and expanded for use at follow-ups, and since the questions at the two follow-ups were identical, the same scheme was used for both. A number of categories were, however, added to each of the three questions asked, to take account of additional points or issues raised at this stage, as follows:

Question 1.

13. I received help and support
14. I was able to spend more time with my child
15. I am now on a course of study
16. I now have a part-time job/am helping out in school
17. I am better at speaking in public/in group discussion
18. I am better at communicating/more willing to talk

Question 2.

12. Help more in the house

Question 3.

8. Repeated tasks that we did on the course
9. Visit the library regularly
10. More activities/outings outside home
11. I have started a new course
12. I have started helping in school
13. Helps more in the house

Distribution of responses on Home Activities questionnaire

Notes:

1. The distribution of responses on all items is shown. The figures shown are in all cases **numbers**, not percentages. But the total numbers returned at the various stages were, because of the research design, very different:

Beginning of course	396
End of course	323
12-week follow-up	202
9-month follow-up	93

Comparisons between stages therefore cannot be made on the basis of the **absolute** numbers, only on the basis of the distribution or **pattern** of responses and particularly any **changes** in that pattern.

2. In the first three pages of data,

- *the top line gives the results for the beginning of the course*

- *the second line gives the results for the end of the course*

- *the third line gives the results for the 12-week follow-up, and*

- *the bottom line gives the results for the 9-month follow-up.*

(For the remaining items, see p.157.)

Does your child look at any of these with you at home?	Never	1-2 a year	1-2 a month	1 a week	2-3 a week	Every day
Magazines	68	21	79	112	65	14
	17	14	52	88	85	28
	8	8	29	66	46	22
	5	2	15	25	28	8
Catalogues	27	54	117	68	67	34
	16	26	74	59	89	28
	7	13	52	44	51	13
	1	10	30	18	17	4
Newspapers	202	21	29	42	31	28
	62	10	48	59	44	64
	41	10	24	35	22	42
	16	1	10	21	10	24
TV Guide	168	9	24	53	35	62
	70	9	19	71	39	76
	40	4	13	34	27	60
	22	3	7	11	7	31
Labels on food packets	56	9	46	75	71	100
	10	3	20	46	80	131
	7	2	8	26	51	86
	2	0	4	15	19	45
Letters	113	46	57	43	42	58
	33	25	56	49	60	64
	20	14	37	29	47	31
	8	6	13	16	22	16
Books	2	1	7	20	88	254
	1	1	3	8	42	245
	0	1	1	1	23	157
	0	1	0	1	9	73
Photo albums	10	110	154	44	33	21
	4	59	129	46	39	21
	2	34	86	27	27	8
	1	19	40	13	7	4
Religious material	239	54	27	28	4	3
	151	62	24	38	8	3
	87	39	25	20	5	3
	37	17	11	13	3	1

Does your child do any of these activities with you?	Never	1-2 a year	1-2 a month	1 a week	2-3 a week	Every day
Write a shopping list	200	19	52	76	11	3
	65	12	55	132	29	3
	34	12	37	82	11	4
	13	1	19	33	12	3
Help with shopping	6	4	55	191	77	38
	2	5	35	128	93	36
	2	2	20	95	39	27
	1	1	9	38	18	17
Write his/her name	42	4	18	61	94	145
	10	1	4	24	77	184
	5	1	6	9	44	120
	2	0	3	8	16	54
Drawing/painting	16	2	23	64	119	142
	2	1	0	21	89	183
	1	0	5	16	50	112
	1	1	5	9	21	46
Use a computer	163	19	46	62	42	31
	86	15	48	53	56	31
	51	7	25	41	39	16
	22	4	15	13	20	8
Play with:						
– make believe toys	55	14	41	55	75	124
	21	7	17	35	62	151
	9	2	17	24	44	87
	8	2	6	13	19	36
– jigsaws	32	23	99	86	89	38
	10	11	60	76	96	42
	7	7	45	33	59	29
	1	6	24	15	29	10
– cutting and sticking	44	23	81	100	90	31
	6	2	43	73	110	63
	4	5	36	44	67	27
	1	6	18	16	27	16
– making a scrapbook	215	45	54	27	18	6
	64	55	78	53	30	15
	38	42	58	31	12	2
	16	17	29	10	8	5

Does your child do any of these with you?	Never	1-2 a year	1-2 a month	1 a week	2-3 a week	Every day
Watch TV	2	1	3	19	52	299
	1	0	1	7	25	266
	1	0	1	2	17	164
	1	0	0	1	11	72
Talk about TV	22	2	15	39	98	191
	3	1	6	20	58	210
	1	1	0	12	48	122
	1	0	0	9	19	56
Listen to stories you make up	73	28	83	79	69	35
	23	12	45	80	86	45
	12	11	31	41	51	33
	9	4	16	15	24	14
Make up stories for you	68	17	66	86	73	52
	24	5	35	75	92	61
	12	6	30	27	57	49
	6	3	14	12	26	21
Use the telephone (real or toy)	20	9	38	75	124	101
	16	3	35	49	101	96
	7	2	17	30	79	50
	3	0	6	12	38	26
Play schools	106	22	57	64	64	48
	37	7	42	60	79	60
	18	7	36	41	50	30
	6	3	14	15	28	18
Sing songs	13	4	28	44	99	180
	3	1	9	24	51	210
	0	0	7	12	37	126
	0	0	7	7	12	59
Tell nursery rhymes	21	9	52	67	116	102
	5	2	28	45	83	135
	6	5	24	16	59	74
	2	3	13	9	26	32
Tell you what happened at school	24	0	8	26	79	234
	16	1	3	12	52	216
	7	0	2	10	19	145
	2	0	1	4	5	71
Go on an outing	4	27	119	136	66	18
	1	19	80	114	66	17
	1	13	54	71	41	5
	0	5	20	36	19	5

For the remaining six items,

- *the left-hand column gives the results for the **beginning** of the course*

- *the second column gives the results for the **end** of the course*

- *the third column gives the results for the **12-week follow-up**, and*

- *the right-hand column gives the results for the **9-month follow-up**.*

How many children's books does your child have of his/her own?				
None	1	0	0	0
1 or 2 books	4	1	0	0
3 to 9 books	25	11	8	4
10 to 19 books	70	32	13	4
20 to 49 books	121	106	57	23
50 or more	152	151	106	54

How often do you read stories to your child?				
Never	5	2	0	1
Several times a year	7	2	0	1
Several times a month	33	9	7	6
Once a week	46	22	13	6
At least 3 times a week	140	82	49	24
Every day	142	184	116	46

Do you borrow children's books from the library?				
Never	162	73	43	12
1 – 2 a year	34	21	12	4
1 – 2 a month	110	124	79	38
1 a week	35	48	30	16
2 – 3 a week	26	30	17	12
Every day	3	4	4	2

How often do you go to school activities?				
Never	51	15	8	2
1 – 2 a year	155	122	78	34
1 – 2 a month	67	74	58	26
1 a week	41	43	10	6
2 – 3 a week	32	36	21	13

How often do you help with school activities?				
Never	168	94	56	15
1 – 2 a year	81	82	59	23
1 – 2 a month	29	36	20	15
1 a week	24	40	18	10
2 – 3 a week	31	30	16	11
Every day	8	11	11	6

How often do you talk with the child's teacher?				
Never	22	6	3	0
1 – 2 a year	41	22	12	7
1 – 2 a month	70	58	25	10
1 a week	82	57	40	20
2 – 3 a week	62	59	39	18
Every day	77	90	63	27

Child and adult profiles

―――――――

Family Literacy Demonstration Programmes

Child Profile

Identifier ⌊_⌊_⌊_⌊_⌊_⌋ 6 - 11

Gender 12

☐ Female   ☐ Male

Date of Birth 13 - 18

⌊_⌊_/⌊_⌊_/⌊_⌊_⌋

Time in UK 14 - 22

⌊_⌊_⌋ years   ⌊_⌊_⌋ months

Ethnic Group 23

1 ☐ White
2 ☐ Black – Caribbean
3 ☐ Black – African

4 ☐ Black – other
5 ☐ Indian
6 ☐ Pakistani

7 ☐ Bangladeshi
8 ☐ Chinese
9 ☐ Other (please specify)

⌊_____⌋

Languages

	understood	spoken	literate	
⌊_____⌋	☐	☐	☐	24 - 27
⌊_____⌋	☐	☐	☐	28 - 31
⌊_____⌋	☐	☐	☐	32 - 35
⌊_____⌋	☐	☐	☐	36 - 39

Family Literacy Demonstration Programmes

Adult Profile

Identifier |⎵|⎵|⎵|⎵|⎵|⎵| 6 - 11

Gender 12	Date of Birth 13 - 18	Time in UK 14 - 22
☐ Female ☐ Male	|⎵|⎵| / |⎵|⎵| / |⎵|⎵|	|⎵|⎵| years |⎵|⎵| months

Ethnic Group   23

1 ☐ White   4 ☐ Black – other   7 ☐ Bangladeshi

2 ☐ Black – Caribbean   5 ☐ Indian   8 ☐ Chinese

3 ☐ Black – African   6 ☐ Pakistani   9 ☐ Other (please specify)

Occupational Status   24

1 ☐ Full-time paid employee   5 ☐ Unemployed   9 ☐ Looking after home/family

2 ☐ Part-time paid employee   6 ☐ Full-time education   0 ☐ Other (please specify)

3 ☐ Full-time self employed   7 ☐ Temporarily sick/disabled

4 ☐ Part-time self employed   8 ☐ Permanently sick/disabled

Children   25

Identifier	Date of birth
|⎵|⎵|⎵|⎵|⎵|⎵|	|⎵|⎵| / |⎵|⎵| / |⎵|⎵|
|⎵|⎵|⎵|⎵|⎵|⎵|	|⎵|⎵| / |⎵|⎵| / |⎵|⎵|
|⎵|⎵|⎵|⎵|⎵|⎵|	|⎵|⎵| / |⎵|⎵| / |⎵|⎵|
|⎵|⎵|⎵|⎵|⎵|⎵|	|⎵|⎵| / |⎵|⎵| / |⎵|⎵|
|⎵|⎵|⎵|⎵|⎵|⎵|	|⎵|⎵| / |⎵|⎵| / |⎵|⎵|
|⎵|⎵|⎵|⎵|⎵|⎵|	|⎵|⎵| / |⎵|⎵| / |⎵|⎵|
|⎵|⎵|⎵|⎵|⎵|⎵|	|⎵|⎵| / |⎵|⎵| / |⎵|⎵|

Languages

	understood	spoken	literate
_____	☐	☐	☐ 26 - 29
_____	☐	☐	☐ 30 - 33
_____	☐	☐	☐ 34 - 37
_____	☐	☐	☐ 38 - 41

Education

Highest qualification awarded |_____| 42

Education in UK

Years in full-time education |⎵⎵| Was this continuous? ☐ Yes   ☐ No (please expand)   45
    43 - 44

_____

_____

_____

Education outside UK

Years in full-time education |⎵⎵| Was this continuous? ☐ Yes   ☐ No (please expand)   48
    46 - 47

_____

_____

_____

Previous basic skills tuition   ☐ Yes   ☐ No   49

Cloze tests

Test 1

Please fill in the gaps with words which you think make sense.

My daughter _____ to copy me. When she _____
          (likes)   *(plays)*

with her doll she likes _____ dress it up. She talks to
                           (to)

_____ and tells it what to _____. Sometimes my
      (it)   *(do)*

son _____ me wash the dishes. We put lots _____
    (helps)   *(of)*

water in the sink. He enjoys making bubbles. _____ we
                                          (When)

finish washing and drying _____ dishes we put them
                            (the)

_____ away. Sometimes he _____ bored before
    (all)   *(gets)*

we finish.

Test 2

Please fill in the gaps with words which you think make sense.

Before children go to school they are learning many things which

help them learn to read. They _____ learning to read at
(start)

home. It _____ never too early to start. Even before
(is)

_____ can sit up, babies will listen to _____ sound
(they)   *(the)*

of words as you _____ to them. They enjoy it when
(talk)

_____ sing to them and tell them _____ or nursery
(you)   *(stories)*

rhymes.

Little children like books _____ pictures, there do not have
(with)

_____ be any words. They enjoy _____ the noises of
(to)   *(making)*

animals they see _____ the pictures. But there are words for
(in)

_____ to learn about in many other places _____
(them)   *(not)*

just in books. They are _____ the Cornflakes box and on the
(on)

labels of _____ of food. They are also on the _____
(tins)   *(signs)*

you see when you walk down _____ road.
(the)

Test 3

Please fill in the gaps with words which you think make sense.

County School
London Road
Weston
E16 4LL

Dear Parents

This term your child's class will be working on the topic of "Animals".

As _____ of this work the children _____ Year 1
      (part)   *(in)*

classes will be _____ a visit to Calcot Hall Farm _____
           (making)   *(in)*

Brentwood on May 5th. The farm has _____ variety of
                                            (a)

animals and there will be opportunities for the _____ to
                                            (children)

learn about their care, diet, _____ the overall management
                               (and)

of a small farm.

The children _____ be travelling by coach and will be
               (will)

_____ the school at 9.15 am and returning _____
   (leaving)   *(not)*

later than 2.30 pm. They will be _____ by the Year 1 class
                                (accompanied)

teachers. If _____ child suffers from travel sickness
               (your)

_____ ensure that they take any necessary _____
   (please)   *(medicine)*

before coming to school. Your child will _____ a packed
                                   (need)

lunch. For safety reasons _____ should not be any glass
                           (there)

containers.

Please make _____ (sure) that your child has suitable clothes

_____ (for) this trip. Even in May it can _____ (be) quite cold

when the children are _____ (out) of doors for a period of time

and they _____ (will) need some warm clothing. As the

_____ (farm) is likely to be muddy, they should not _____ (wear)

clothes which are likely to _____ (be) spoilt.

If any _____ (mums) or dads would like to join us and help

_____ (with) this trip we are able to include a small _____ (number)

of adults. Please talk to your _____ (child's) class teacher if you are

_____ (interested) So that we have your _____ (permission) for your child to

take part in this outing, I enclose a consent _____ (form) Please

complete this and return _____ (it) to your child's class teacher

_____ (by) April 20.

I hope that your _____ (child) enjoys the trip and finds it

interesting.

Yours sincerely

Headteacher

Parent interview schedules

INTERVIEW SCHEDULE FOR PARENTS – FOR USE DURING COURSE

Group of participants: Summer 94 / Autumn 94 / Spring 95 / Summer 95

Parent's name: _____ ID _____

Programme: _____ Date: _____ Interviewer: _____

A.   Background data:

Ethnic group: First language:

1. How did you come to know about the Family Literacy Programme?
    (N.B. Use local title.)

2. How old is/are your own child(ren)? (give names and ages of all children, both those participating
    and those not)

3. Why did you decide to take part in the programme?

B.   Benefit to parent

4. Have you enjoyed taking part in the programme so far?

5. What parts of the programme have you found most interesting?

6. Was there anything that was not very interesting? (Prompt for examples)

7. What have you found most useful? (Prompt for examples)

8. Do you think that you have personally benefited from the programme so far? (Prompt: In
    particular, in what ways has the programme benefited your own reading and writing?)

9. Could you give me an example of something you have learnt? (Prompt: Can you give me more
    examples of what you have learnt about reading and writing?)

10. Since you started this programme, have you changed anything about reading materials you keep
    at home? (Prompt: Can you give me more examples? Continue to ask this until the parent can't
    think of any more examples.)

11. Since you started this programme, have you changed anything about the kinds of reading and writing your children see you do? (Prompt: Can you give me more examples? Continue to ask this until the parent can't think of any more examples.)

12. Have you learnt anything from other parents in the group?

C.   Joint activities with child(ren)

13. Have you learnt things that have helped you to teach your child (use name) reading or writing?

14. Could you give me some examples of how you have been able to help (child – use name) in reading?

15. And can you give me some examples of how you have been able to help (child – use name) in writing?

16. And can you give me some examples of how you have been able to help (child – use name) in talking?

17. Has this benefited your other children's reading or writing or talking? Can you give me some examples?

D.   Parent's opinions of programme

18. Have you found any aspects of the programme difficult; for example, things relating to the **timetable** or **organisation, what** was taught or the **way** it was taught?

> timetable/organisation
>
> content of teaching (what was taught)
>
> methods (how it was taught)
>
> other

19. In general, do you think the programme has been successful, so far?

20. Do you think it would be helpful to parents if there were more programmes like the one you have been involved in?

E.   Plans

21. What do you plan to do as a result of the programme when you've completed it?

22. Are there any other comments you would like to make about the programme?

F.   Activity scales
Finally, can I ask you a few questions about how often you do certain literacy activities with (participating child's name)?

A   In the last week, how many times has (child) seen you reading or writing?

> 0   1   2   3   4   5   6   7   8   9   – – – –

B How does this compare with before the programme? Is it more often, about the same, or less often?

    Please circle one: More often / about same / less often

C In the last week, how many times has (child) shared a book with you?

    0   1   2   3   4   5   6   7   8   9   ----

D How does this compare with before the programme? Is it more often, about the same, or less often?

    Please circle one: More often / about same / less often

E In the last week, how many times has (child) asked you to read to him/her?

    0   1   2   3   4   5   6   7   8   9   ----

F How does this compare with before the programme? Is it more often, about the same, or less often?

    Please circle one: More often / about same / less often

G In the last week, how many times has (child) scribbled, printed, made letters, or written AT HOME?

    0   1   2   3   4   5   6   7   8   9   ----

H How does this compare with before the programme? Is it more often, about the same, or less often?

    Please circle one: More often / about same / less often

I In the last **month**, how many times have you taken (child) to the library?

    0   1   2   3   4   5   6   7   8   9   ----

J How does this compare with before the programme? Is it more often, about the same, or less often?

    Please circle one: More often / about same / less often

INTERVIEW SCHEDULE FOR PARENTS – FOR USE AT 12-WEEK FOLLOW-UP

Group of participants: Summer 94 / Autumn 94 / Spring 95

Parent's name: _____ **ID** _____

Programme: _____ **Date:** _____ **Interviewer:** _____

N.B. Use local title of programme throughout.

1. When the programme ended, what did you plan to do as a result of it?

2. How have those plans worked out so far? (Prompt for detail.)

3. Do you think you are continuing to benefit from the programme? Please give examples.

4. Do you think your child(ren) is/are continuing to benefit from the programme? Please give examples. (Prompt for detail, especially on children's confidence as well as literacy.)

5. Do you have more confidence about your own reading and writing now, as a result of the course, and about helping your children? (Prompt for detail, especially about joint sessions.)

6. Do you think you know more now about how children learn to read and write? (Prompt for detail.)

7. Looking back now at the programme, what do you think was the most useful thing about it? Please give examples.

8. And still looking back at the programme, would you have wanted anything to be different about it? Please give examples.

9. What do you plan to do from now on as a result of the programme?

10. Are there any other comments you'd like to make about the programme?

INTERVIEW SCHEDULE FOR PARENTS – FOR USE AT 9-MONTH FOLLOW-UP

Group of participants: Summer 94 / Autumn 94

Parent's name: _____ **ID** _____

Programme: _____ **Date:** _____ **Interviewer:** _____

N.B. Use local title of programme throughout.

1. Do you think your child(ren) is/are continuing to benefit from the programme? Please give examples. (Prompt for detail, especially on children's confidence as well as literacy.)

2. Please tell me about the literacy activities you carry out now with your children).

3. Have you had any feedback from your child(ren)'s teacher about their progress? (If Yes:) Please give me details, especially on their reading and writing.

4. Do you think your reading and writing are continuing to benefit from the programme? Please give examples.

5. Do you think you are continuing to benefit in other ways from the programmes? Please give details.

6. Since our discussion 6 months ago, to what extent have you been involved in your child(ren)'s school?

7. And since our discussion 6 months ago, how have your plans for further courses worked out? (Prompt for detail.)

8. Do you think it would be helpful to parents if there were more programmes like the one you have been involved in? Why (not)?

9. Do you still have plans for things to do as a result of the programme? (If Yes:) Please tell me about them.

10. Are there any other comments you'd like to make about the programme?

Coordinator interview schedules

FIRST INTERVIEW SCHEDULE FOR COORDINATORS – SUMMER TERM 1994

Coordinator: _____ **Role:** Adult / Early Years

Programme: _____ **Date:** _____ **Interviewer:** _____

A. Initial Stages

1. Could you please tell me why you have a particular interest in family literacy?

2. When did you become aware of the Agency's family literacy initiative?

3. Who were the people most involved in the initiation of your programme?

4. Can you outline your own involvement in the programme up to its formal start?

5. What were the main difficulties you encountered during the initial stages of the programme?

B. The Recruitment Process

I would like to get some information about the methods used to publicise the programme and to 'recruit' parents:

6. Can you give me some information about the methods used to publicise the programme?

7. What methods were used to make contact with parents?

8. How did you decide which schools to involve in the programme?

9. To what extent did you involve teachers in making contact with parents?

10. How did parents respond to the publicity? (Please give the approximate numbers of those who responded in the reception year, year 1, year 2 and pre-reception.)

11. Did you organise separate introductory sessions for parents of children of different ages?

12. Is there any other information you would like to give me about activities leading up to the main programme?

C. The Main Programme

13. Could you give me some details about the organisation of the programme for parents and children in the 1994 summer term. (I'd be grateful if you could let me have a copy of a timetable for the sessions.)

14. In general terms how does the programme differ from previous programmes?

15. What would you say are the main emphases in the teaching programme for **parents**?

16. Could you give me some examples of the types of activities employed with parents?

17. What are the main emphases in the instructional programme for **children**?

18. Again, could you give me some examples of the activities you used?

19. What are the main emphases in the **joint** sessions?

20. Can you give me some examples of the activities used?

21. Which of the activities (in each of the programmes) did you think were the most successful?

D. Evaluation/Review

22. In your view what aspects of the programme have been most successful or effective to date, e.g. with respect to:
    a) setting up the programme
    b) recruitment and retention of parents
    c) the teaching programme for parents
    d) the teaching programme for children
    e) the joint sessions
    f) other

23. What aspects, if any, have been least effective?
    a) setting up the programme
    b) recruitment and retention of parents
    c) the teaching programme for parents
    d) the teaching programme for children
    e) the joint sessions

24. Are there any other comments you would like to make about the programme?

SECOND INTERVIEW SCHEDULE FOR COORDINATORS – AUTUMN TERM 1994

Coordinator: _____ **Role:** Adult / Early Years

Programme: _____ **Date:** _____ **Interviewer:** _____

A.   Progress of Summer 1994 groups

1.   Can you please tell me how you are keeping in touch with the summer 1994 parents?

2.   What plans did they have for after their course, and how have those plans worked out?

3.   Have any of those parents been involved in recruitment for this term?

4.   (a) Have any of last term's children started school this term?
     (b) Have you had any feedback from their teachers?
     (c) What about feedback on children involved last term who were already in school?
     (d) And on other children in the families?

5.   How involved are last term's parents with their children's schools now? How does this compare with their involvement earlier?

6.   What would you say are last term's parents' aspirations for their children's attainment/progress in school? How do you think this compares with their aspirations earlier?

B.   Autumn 1994 groups

7.   I understand that all the programmes have expanded this term. Can you give me some details of the expansion here? (Prompt: new sites, new staff, numbers of parents and children)

8.   How has recruitment gone this term? What methods did you use to publicise the programme, and to what extent did they differ from last term's?

9.   Before I go today, can you let me have a copy of this term's timetable, for this site at least? Have you changed the timetable materially since last term?

10. Have you changed your teaching approach materially since last term? (If Yes:) Can you give me details of the changes, and of why you made them?

C.   Broader issues

11. The Agency's framework sets the broad shape of all the programmes, but within that you have had choices to make about the **content** and approach you would use. Can you tell me about the choices of content that you have made for the sessions for **parents alone/children alone**, and why you made those choices? (Prompt: What impact do you expect these activities to make on parents'/children's literacy, and why?)

12. And can you tell me about the choices of **teaching approach** that you have made for the sessions for **parents alone/children alone**, and why you made those choices? (Prompt: What impact do you expect these activities to make on parents'/children's literacy, and why?)

13. Now I'd like you to tell me about the **joint** sessions. Can you tell about the choices of **content** that you have made for those sessions, and why you made those choices? (Prompt: What impact do you expect these activities to make on parents' **and** children's literacy, and why?)

14. And still thinking about the **joint** sessions, can you tell me about the choices of **teaching approach** that you have made for those sessions, and why you made those choices? (Prompt: What impact do you expect these activities to make on parents' and children's literacy, and why?)

15. Are there any other comments you'd like to make at ths stage?

THIRD INTERVIEW SCHEDULE FOR COORDINATORS – SPRING TERM 1995

Coordinator: _____   **Role:** Adult / Early Years

Programme: _____   Date: _____   Interviewer: _____

A. Progress of Summer and Autumn 1994 groups

1. What news have you of the summer 1994 parents? In particular,
   – to what extent has their involvement in their children's school continued?
   – to what extent have their plans for further courses worked out?
   – how are plans going for the 9-month follow-up in May this year?

2. Can you please tell me how you are keeping in touch with the autumn 1994 parents?

3. What plans did the autumn 1994 parents have for after their course, and how have those plans worked out?

4. Have any of the autumn 1994 parents been involved in recruitment for this term's courses?

5. (a) Have any of last term's children started school this term?
   (b) Have you had any feedback from their teachers?
   (c) What about feedback on children involved last term who were already in school?
   (d) And on other children in the families?

6. How involved are last term's parents with their children's schools now? How does this compare with their involvement earlier?

7. What would you say are last term's parents' aspirations for their children's attainment/progress in school? How do you think this compares with their aspirations earlier?

B. Spring 1995 groups

8. Can you give me outline details of your courses this term? (Prompt: number of courses, numbers of parents and children, which sites, new sites, state of premises.
   N.B. Keep back details of new staff until q.13.)

9. How has recruitment gone this term? What methods did you use to publicise the programme, and to what extent did they differ from last term's?

10. Before I go today, can you let me have a copy of this term's timetable, for this site at least? Have you changed the timetable materially since last term?

11. Have you changed your teaching approach materially since last term? (If Yes:) Can you give me details of the changes, and of why you made them?

C.   Successes and Challenges

12. (If needed as a result of q.8.)
    How has expansion, or any change of site, affected the Programme?

13. Please give details of the retention, turnover and recruitment of staff, especially any new staff. Can you tell me how new staff have adapted to the Programme? How have the new approaches/ideas of new staff fitted in/contributed?

14. What training needs have you identified for yourself and/or for other Programme staff? To what extent have these been met?

15. What progress has there been in the logistics of transporting equipment between sites? Have you had any other logistical problems?

16. What would you say was the impact of having creche facilities on the effectiveness of the Programme?

17. What would you say was the impact of having transport facilities on the effectiveness of the Programme?

18. To what extent have you been able to make schools aware of the facilities and equipment you need when they agree to have one of your courses on their premises? And to what extent have schools agreed to the amount of access to the children that you need?

19. In general, how effective has the collaboration with schools been?

20. In general, how effective has the collaboration between Adult and Early Years staff in the Programme been?

21. In general, how effective has the collaboration between Programme staff and your line management authority been?

22. To what extent have you found the Agency's model of Family Literacy helpful, and appropriate to your Programme's circumstances?

23. To what extent have you found the meetings with the other Programmes at the Agency helpful?

24. What would you say are the major challenges you face in implementing the Programme at the moment?

25. We (the NFER team) think the Demonstration Programmes have been very successful. What would you say are the main factors in that success? (Prompt in particular for process factors, e.g. quality of teaching, responsiveness of staff to parents' and children's needs, growth in parents' confidence, etc., but without suggesting any.)

26. Are there any other comments you'd like to make at this stage?

FOURTH INTERVIEW SCHEDULE FOR COORDINATORS – SUMMER TERM 1995

Coordinator: _____   **Role:** Adult / Early Years

Programme: _____   Date: _____   Interviewer: _____

A. Recruitment

1. On recruitment, we get the impression that in the early days when you were talking to potential parent participants you all stressed the benefits for their children. To what extent has this changed over time? (Probe extent to which they have felt able to be more upfront with parents about benefit they would derive, without risk of suggesting that parents' skills are deficient.)

2. On recruitment again, in later terms have you been able to recruit more Foundation level parents than at the beginning? If so, has this been because of changes in the way you went about recruitment?

3. And still on recruitment, how has the balance altered over the terms between direct approach by you and your colleagues versus encouragement from previous participants?

4. Looking back over the 4 or 5 terms that the Programme has been operating, have you noticed any significant differences between the cohorts, that is the different terms' groups of participants? This could be in terms of starting point, motivation, progress, etc. (Probe on differences in parents' and children's initial literacy levels and parents' previous qualifications; differences between central/continuing sites and changing/new ones.)

B. Benefit to parents

5. Most participants have lived within walking distance of their course site, and most course activities have taken place there. Can you give me a picture of (a) how transport has been arranged for participants who live beyond walking distance of their course site, and (b) separately, how transport has been arranged for any course activities which have taken place beyond walking distance from the course site? What has been the effect of transport provision on the Programme's success?

6. (Adult Coordinators only) One important measure of the effectiveness of the Programmes is the progress the parents make with their own literacy, and it's clear that the proportion of parents who achieve Wordpower accreditation is impressive. But we need to have some idea of how that progress compares with the progress people make on conventional stand-alone Adult Basic Education courses, that is ABE courses without the Family Literacy element. In your judgment as an experienced ABE tutor, how does the progress in literacy made by parents in this Family Literacy Programme compare with that of adults on ordinary ABE courses? What yardstick can you use for this? (Probe on attendance and retention; also on accreditation, including length of time taken to acquire it.)

7. An implicit objective of the Programmes is to make a difference to the participating parents' lives. Perhaps the most measurable aspect of that is the further courses they go on to, and the Programmes' success in that respect is logged in the destination statistics. But we'd like to get

some sense also of the less measurable differences that the Programmes have made to parents' lives. Can you tell me what you've noticed about these more imponderable life changes? (Probe on jobs, relations with schools, 'more abundant life'.)

8. Where participating parents are concerned, the Programmes have dual aims, namely to boost parents' own skills and to boost their ability to foster their children's development. How successful do you think your Programme has been in maintaining a balance between these two aims? And how effective do you think your Programme has been in achieving these two aims in relation to each other?

C.   Teaching

9. The Programmes all subscribe to the principle that they should follow, or at least be responsive to, the parents' agenda. On the other hand, the Agency's model sets some fairly firm parameters. So, in detail, to what extent are you able to adapt the courses in line with the parents' wishes? (Probe for examples of the tutors' agenda having been modified, and on the extent to which, if at all, this stretched the Agency's and/or the tutors' own parameters.)

10. In all education there is a gap between what teachers intend to do and what actually goes on. How large do you think this gap has been in your Programme? Has it changed over the life of the Programme? What would you have liked to do that there was insufficient time for? (Probe for examples.)

11. In your view, how coherent has the programme for the children been? What was the rationale of the Early Years teaching?

12. To what extent is parents reading with their children an activity during joint sessions? Can you tell me what impression you have gained of the quality of the interaction between parents and children while this is going on, and how this changes during the courses?

13. Looking back over the 4 or 5 terms that the Programme has been operating, what do you think have been the most successful teaching activities or aspects of your Programme? (Probe for specifics within activities, e.g. computer use, phonics.)

14. Again, looking back over the 4 or 5 terms that the Programme has been operating, what do you think have been the least successful teaching activities or aspects of your Programme? Or to put that another way, what would you do differently if you were starting again?

D.   The Family Literacy model

Now I'd like to ask you a series of 7 questions about the Agency's model of Family Literacy. In each case, please tell me how well you think that aspect of the model has worked, and why.

15. So first, the amount of time, the 80+ hours:

16. Secondly, the fact that the Programmes had joint Adult and Early Years staffing:

17. Thirdly, the fact that the Adult and Early years staff were engaged in joint planning:

18. Fourthly, the fact that there were joint sessions for parents and children:

19. Fifthly, the fact that there was an accreditation framework for the parents:

20. Sixthly, the fact that the courses were intensive. How might they have worked if they had been, say, 3 hours a week for a year instead of 8 hours a week for 12 weeks?

21. Finally (on this topic), how well has the model worked, in your opinion?

22. What factors would you identify as contributing to your Programme's success? (Probe for factors external to the courses and internal to the courses.)

E. The future

23. Can you tell me what plans you have for when the Programme funding ends?

24. In particular, what are the prospects for Family Literacy-type courses being delivered by either an Adult tutor or an Early Years tutor on her own if she hasn't been involved in this type of joint course? Or in the absence of a crèche? Or if rent had to be paid for premises? What is the appropriate student/teacher ratio? Which features of the teaching do you think would be replicable in other settings?

25. Are there any other comments you'd like to make?

Observation schedule

───────

Observation System

This page contains general information on the system, and (unlike the pages of the observation schedule itself) is not intended for making notes.

In these notes and the schedule, the term 'students' is used to mean 'parents or children or both', as appropriate.

Before each observation, see the tutor and agree your non-participant stance. That is, not only are you not a participant in the session, but you are also not there as a 'connoisseur' – the tutor should not expect evaluation or advice from you afterwards. You are there as a neutral recorder, and will be making notes of as much of the interaction as possible.

If possible make a sketch of the room and its layout. Note display and equipment, and anything of interest about 'atmosphere'.

During every session observed, keep a detailed log. However, there is no need to code the interactions – since we shall be collecting at most 16 observations on each type of session (parents only/children only/joint), such micro-detail will not be useful. What is needed is a running record of what is happening, especially tutor moves and the interaction.

While observing and keeping a log, do not begin filling in the judgments to be made after the session. However, judgments arising from the current situation should be noted in the log. When the log is typed up, such judgments should be distinguished from the log itself by being in bold type and placed in brackets.

Substantive judgments are to be made after the session and to address the issues in part 4 of the schedule.

All observations are to be written up.

It is recognised that not all information can be collected on every session observed - just collect as much as is feasible.

If the answer to any question is 'not applicable', enter 'n/a'.

OBSERVATION SCHEDULE

1. Background data

Observer .... Date..

Times: Start of session... End of session ....

Programme ....

Location ....

Type of session: Parents only / children only / joint

Tutor ....

Number of people present: parents .... children ....

Was anyone present other than the relevant tutor, the students and you? If so, note here who they were and their role in the session:

2. Before the session

See the tutor. You may not be able to talk to her for very long - if so, just ask the first question; the rest can be picked up afterwards.

Ask the tutor:

- – What are you planning to do with the parents/children today?
- – What is the general purpose to the lesson?
- – What are the specific aims?
- – How does this relate to what the parents/children have done previously?
- – Is there anything it would be helpful for me to know about particular parents/children in the group?

Collect any relevant documentation and tick below those obtained:

    i.   scheme of work
    ii.   lesson plan
    iii. stimulus material
    iv.   other (specify (..)

Tutor's guidance to support staff (if any):

3. During the session

Keep a detailed log - see the introductory sheet.

4. Judgments on the session

A   Purpose and direction

    In what ways was the teaching purposeful?
    e.g. Were the objectives clear? Were they explained to the students? Were they covered?

B   Interest and motivation

How did the activities create and sustain interest and motivation?
e.g. Was the content introduced with skill and imagination? What strategies were used to assist students to complete the work?

C   Resources

What resources were used? Were they appropriate for the purpose? Were they appropriate for the students? Were they used effectively?

D   Appropriateness to needs/abilities

How did the session cater for different abilities and needs?
e.g. In what way was the content appropriate to students' understanding? Was the teaching style appropriate for parents and/or children? What strategies were used to help those who did not succeed at their first attempt?

E   Management

How was the session managed to ensure that all involved learnt something?
e.g. Were any support staff effectively deployed? Did only a few individuals contribute actively?

F   Interaction

In what ways was there effective interaction between participants (i.e., as appropriate, between tutor and students/among parents/among children/ between parents and children)?
e.g. Was the session mainly tutor-led? Did those who wished to get an opportunity to contribute? In joint sessions, did parents communicate only with their own child?

G   Continuity and Progression

How did the session gear with longer-term objectives of the tutor and the course?
e.g. How did the session relate to previous activities? Did the session point to or suggest further activities to reinforce or apply what was learnt?

General or Further Comments

especially on what made the session effective for teaching literacy:
(parents' sessions) What did the parents learn that would help with their own literacy?
(children's sessions) What did the children learn that would help develop their literacy?
(joint sessions) What did the parents learn that would help them develop their children's literacy?

5. After the session

See the tutor. Collect any further relevant documentation, e.g. samples of students' work. In a discussion with the tutor, concentrate on the following questions:

Delivery

How do you feel the session went today?

Did you get through what you wanted to cover?

Would you say, in terms of the teaching (and despite my presence), that it was a fairly typical session?

Were there any particularly difficult moments for you, the tutor (e.g. pressure of time/from other students), and were there any times when things seemed to be going particularly well?

Purpose

What do you think were the most successful activities?

Were there any that didn't work as well as you had hoped?

What particularly did you want the students to learn/experience?

Did this happen?

Motivation

Were you pleased with the way the parents/children responded to what they were asked to do?

Were there any parents/children who found it difficult to do what they asked to do?

How effective do you think the session was in catering for differing abilities?

Interaction

Did the parents/children contribute as much to the session as you hoped?

Was there anyone who didn't make a contribution?

Was there as much interaction among/between the parents/children as you had intended?

Progression

(If not asked before the session) How did this session follow on from previous ones?

Can you say at this stage what work might follow on from today?

How do you keep track of what the parents/children learn, and how they make progress?

It's difficult to gauge changes in knowledge and peformance, but have you observed any changes in **attitudes** among the parents/children?

Are there particular parents/children who seem to have benefited noticeably from the programme? In what ways?

Any other comments?

Teachers' impressions questionnaire

1. Name of school ....
2. Teacher's name ....
3. Pupil's name ....
4. Pupil's ID ....
5. Have this pupil's parents been in contact with you/the school more often than / about as often as / less often than you would have expected?

    Please circle one: more often / about as often / less often

    On the pupil's progress in **speaking**:
6. Has this been better than average / about average / below average for pupils of that age in your class?

    Please circle one: better / about average / below

7. Has this been better than you would have expected / about what you would have expected / below what you would have expected of this child from your impressions of him/her early in the term?

    Please circle one: better / about as expected / below

    On the pupil's progress in **reading**:
8. Has this been better than average / about average / below average for pupils of that age in your class?

    Please circle one: better / about average / below

9. Has this been better than you would have expected / about what you would have expected / below what you would have expected of this child from your impressions of him/her early in the term?

    Please circle one: better / about as expected / below

    On the pupil's progress in **writing**:
10. Has this been better than average / about average / below average for pupils of that age in your class?

    Please circle one: better / about average / below

11. I las this been better than you would have expected / about what you would have expected / below what you would have expected of this child from your impressions of him/her early in the term?

    Please circle one: better / about as expected / below